Stones in the Millpond

Previous publication by the author:

Spindrift
Published 1989 – ISBN 0 9515 483 0 1

Stones in the Millpond

by
Christian S. Tait

Published by
Shetland Library
2001

Stones in the Millpond

ISBN 0 904562 50 6

First published by Shetland Library, 2001.

Copyright © Christian S. Tait, 2001

British Library Cataloguing-in-Publication Data
A catalogue record for this book is available from the British Library.

Published by
Shetland Library,
Lower Hillhead,
Lerwick,
Shetland ZE1 0EL, UK.

Printed by
Shetland Litho,
Gremista, Lerwick,
Shetland ZE1 0PX, UK.

CONTENTS

CONTENTS (Continued)

ACKNOWLEDGEMENTS

The author and publishers wish to thank the following for permission to reproduce copyright material:

- Extract (page 100) reprinted from *1914-1918 The Great War and the Shaping of the 20th Century* by Jay Winter and Blain Baggett with permission of BBC Worldwide Limited. Copyright © Community Television of Southern California 1996.

- Cartoons (pages 31 and 33) from *The Best of Fragments from France* by Capt. Bruce Bairnsfather, published by T. & V. Holt Associates, 1998.

- Trench diagram (page 35) reprinted from the 4 Day Ypres/Vimy/Somme tour folder, Holts Tours, Ltd.

- Extract (page 40) from *Major and Mrs Holt's Battlefield Guide to the Somme.*

- Extracts (pages 37 and 49) reprinted from *Never Such Innocence* by Dr. G. M. Stephen, published by Buchan and Enright 1988.

- Extracts (page 71) from *Guide to Australian Battlefields of the Western Front 1916-1918* by John Laffin, published by Kangaroo Press and the Australian War Memorial, 1992.

- Extracts (pages 48 and 128) from *Doing His Bit* by Robert M. Greig, edited by Alec Cluness and published by The Shetland Times Ltd.

- Extract (page 96) from *The Shetland Times*, November 14, 1918.

We should also like to thank:

- John Coutts for photograph on back cover.

- Shetland Museum for photograph on page 117.

- The Imperial War Museum (Photographic Archive) for photographs Q4267, E Aus 4612, E Aus 399, E Aus 4612 reproduced on pages 58, 107, 110 and 119 respectively.

- Harry L. Tait for photographs on pages 11, 26, 58, 62, 67, 77, 79, 80, 81, 84, 85, 86, 92, 107, 114, 115, 122 and 124, and for scanning the letters.

- Bill Thomson for charcoal drawing reproduced behind each Haiku.

Photographs on pages 40, 88, 89 and the front cover are by C. S. Tait.

THANKS

- I wish to thank the Shetland Arts Trust; the Shetland Islands Community Services, Education Department; the Shetland Islands Council Millennium Project and the Shetland Library for their financial support.

- My special thanks to Robert Sim (Education Department) whose enthusiasm got the ball rolling, and to John Hunter (Chief Librarian) whose efforts and expertise as co-editor have nursed the book into print.

- I owe a debt of gratitude to the late Harold Morland (Lancashire poet and scholar) whose interest and example started me writing, and to the late George MacKay Brown for encouragement and for insisting I should not "change my voice" at a time when I felt I ought to.

- Thanks also to all my family for their constant support and practical help – especially my husband, Harry, who came with me on three Battlefield Tours, took the photographs, put in many hours on the computer and made this project a joint venture.

Christian S. Tait
11th Nov. 2000

Hjogaland,
Trondra,
Scalloway,
Shetland,
ZE1 0XL.

FOREWORD

Some years before his death my grandfather gave my mother a box of family letters. Most of these were written to him during the First World War by his brothers, nine of whom were actively involved. Three were killed.

Frankie and Sammy served in the British army, and Peter was an officer on the Northern Lightship s.s. *Pharos*. Six other brothers had emigrated to Australia before the outbreak of war – Tommy, Willie and Bertie served in the Australian Forces; and John (Donnie), Bobby and Jamie were officers on Australian Troopships. Their father was captain of the *s.s. St. Rognvald* throughout the war, which earned him his M.B.E. My grandfather (Lollie) was unfit for service due to tuberculosis.

He wrote regularly to his brothers – entertaining and informative letters – giving them family and local news, and also the broader picture of how the war was progressing as each had knowledge only of the area in which he was involved.

He valued their letters highly and believed their story should be told, but the memories were too painful for him. He therefore gave them to my mother in the hope she would "do something with them", for they spent many hours discussing family history together. She treasured them as a tangible link with her uncles; and, some years before she died, she passed them on to me saying "You'll know what to do with them …"

I didn't at first "know what to do with them". I skim-read them and set them aside, knowing that whatever I finally did would involve a great deal of time and a degree of dedication.

In autumn 1997 I went with my husband for a short break in the Ardennes. It was billed as "a mushroom extravaganza". (This explains the references to fungi in some of the poems). We stayed in Charlesville-Mézières, picked mushrooms in the forest and were taught how to cook them by the hotel chef. It was all rather frivolous, and had nothing to do with the war! However it was not possible to travel through that part of the world without developing a deep awareness of what had happened there. Firstly there was the sheer number of cemeteries and memorials. Secondly our field guide told us as we were about to enter the vast forest that it had been entirely destroyed by shellfire in W.W.1, and that there was no doubt that we would be walking on the remains of the "missing". I found this deeply disturbing.

We also learned that this whole area had been devastated – towns and villages flattened not just once but repeatedly. I was left with enormous sympathy and respect for the people who had the resilience and determination to rebuild them over and over again – often as perfect replicas of the originals, as at Ypres and Cambrai.

I also had tremendous admiration for the farmers who ploughed and replanted these dangerous cratered fields which still yield their annual "Iron Harvest". Parallel with this I found comfort in the regenerative powers of the natural world.

FOREWORD (Continued)

I wondered why I seemed to recognise so many of the place-names … then I remembered that I had read them in the letters. This led to the first of the poems (Signposts).

It also led to a thorough study of the letters, a vast amount of reading and research, three visits to the battlefields of northern France and Belgium, and eventually, to this publication.

It is not a history of the Scott family at war. Photographs, information and quotations from the letters have been included to set the poems in context. "Stones in the Millpond" describes an emotional journey in which I finally come to terms with what I have learned. The Haiku (three-lined poems) are the "stones" – which generated "ripples" in my mind, and the poems which follow them.

This is my tribute to my mother, Kathleen E.A. Robertson (née Scott); to my grandfather, Laurence Gray Scott; to his brothers and all those who have suffered directly or indirectly from the horrors of war.

Legacy

She gave me the box
which once contained laundry.
"You'll know what to do
with this, dear," she said.

I thought of smooth linen,
white shirts, damask napkins,
bundles of collars
and starched tablecloths.

Instead, letters – eager
to let loose the legion
of secrets they'd guarded
for near-ninety years.

Notes scrawled in dugouts,
billets-doux, gossip
and (in precise copperplate)
folds of deep thought.

Faces danced round me,
like motes in the sunlight –
faces I knew
from old photographs.

Whispers and laughter,
hymn-tunes and skinbows,
explosions of shells
and the clatter of guns ...

Attar of Roses,
Macassar-oil, cordite –
and a stench that I'd learn
reeked of trenches and death.

I closed the lid quickly,
holding back history.
Some day in the future
I'd confront the past.

These notes refer to the positions held during the Great War

1. **Peter Scott** 29/12/1882 - 29/6/1955. Fourth son, Chief Officer on the Northern Lighthouse Steamer *Pharos*.
2. **Laurence Gray Scott** (Lollie) 11/8/1879 - 25/1/1960. Third son, my grandfather, manager of Anderson and Co., Lerwick. Unfit for service due to Tuberculosis.
3. **McGowan Gray Scott** (Mackie) 21/7/1877 - 11/1/1942. Second son (twin), employed in Stove and Smith, Lerwick.
4. **Ann Scott** (Annie) 28/3/1884 - 5/3/1951. Only daughter. Married Robert Tulloch, banker; lived in Arbroath.
5. **James Moffat Scott** (Jamie) 11/7/1886 - 31/3/1959. Fifth son, 2nd Officer H.M.Australian Transport s.s. *Oteric*. Ship torpedoed in the Mediterranean in 1915.
6. **Thomas Moffat Scott** (Tommy) 7/11/1890 - 14/7/1918. Seventh son. Corporal 1st Australian Light Horse. Served at Gallipoli and Egypt, killed in the Jordan Valley.
7. **Elizabeth Scott** née Gray 7/10/1855 - 6/4/1907. Wife of Captain John Scott, mother of eleven sons and one daughter.
8. **John Scott** 14/12/1852 - 22/6/1940. Master Mariner. Captain of s.s. *St. Rognvald* throughout the war, for which he was awarded the M.B.E.
9. **Francis Halcrow Scott** (Frankie) 20/10/1892 - 4/4/1917. Eighth son. Sergeant 16th Royal Scots. Served in France. Survived the Battle of the Somme. Killed in the preparations for the Battle of Arras.
10. **Bertram Scott** (Bertie) 9/10/1897 - 1/2/ 1919. Tenth son. Private 7th Battalion Australian Imperial Forces. Served in France. Died as a result of wounds received at the Battle of Strazeele.
11. **Robert Michael Scott** (Bob) 10/10/1894 - ?/1/1978. Ninth son. Third Officer H.M.Australian Transport *Willocro*.
12. **William Scott** (Willie) 3/7/1888 - 25/ 7/ 1958. Sixth son. Sergeant 22nd Battalion A.I.F. Wounded in 1918.
13. **John Scott** (Donnie or Jack) 21/7/1877 - 9/10/1952. Firstborn son, twin with McGowan. Second Officer H.M.Australian Transport *Bakara* (He was at sea when this picture was taken, hence the photograph held by Tommy).

Samuel Hunter Gray Scott (Sammy) was born the year after the picture was taken, 1/11/1899 - 29/5/1981. Eleventh son. Private 4th Gordon Highlanders attached to 2nd/14th London Scottish. Served in France. Wounded in July 1918, gassed in October 1918.

Memories bloom here
Like invisible flowers
Some day I'll pluck them

Northern France

Signposts

The coach speeds smoothly
Past blue and white signposts
Arras, Bapaume, Hazebrouck and Cambrai
I must not allow
These place-names to waken
Thoughts which will mar this gold autumn day.

I must not remember
The bundles of letters,
Family letters I've hidden away
"Don't worry, I'm A.1.,
I'm fit as a fiddle.
A miss is as good as a mile, so they say."

Frank wrote those words
From a farmhouse in Hazebrouck,
Told of the kindness of Mme Decool,
Of clean clothes, home cooking,
The joy of hot water,
Of sleeping on straw with its fresh country smell.

Soon after ... "I write
With regret to inform you
That Sergeant Frank Scott has been killed by a shell.
He lies in a grave
In St. Catherine's, near Arras.
Be proud of your son, for he lived – and died – well."

Or Bertie whose shinbone
Was shattered by shrapnel,
Who died on a troopship, was buried at sea;
Or Sammy who choked
On the poisonous gas;
Willie – shot at Bapaume on the way to Cambrai.

I will not allow
These place-names to waken
Thoughts which will mar our gold autumn day
As the coach speeds smoothly
Past blue and white signposts
Arras, Bapaume, Hazebrouck and Cambrai.

Madame Decool Lucien
à Morbecque
Par Hazebrouck
9:ord

Cher Monsieur

Je suis très heureuse de pouvoir vous apprendre que votre cher frère François à été chez moi en repos pour quinze jours il était très heureux, mais j'ai le regret de vous dire qu'il est parti ce matin, je ne sais pour quel endroit il est en parfaite santé.

Veuillez accepter cher Mr mes Sincères Salutations

Mme Decool

Frankie – 27/2/16

She was an awfully decent woman & can tell you we were sorry when we had to leave. She washed our clothes for us & did many other little deeds to make us comfortable. It was her idea to send the card so I hope you will send one in return as I know she would appreciate it.

Frank's Death

Frank died 4/4/17, killed by a shell during the preparations for the Battle of Arras. The official letter below is dated 5/5/17. One wonders why there was such a delay, but the reason becomes clear when we read the official letter (below) and those from his friend Cpl. Andrew Hamilton (see next page).

5/5/17.

Dear Mr Scott

I am very sorry to have to inform you that 18907 Sergeant Frank Scott was killed by a shell in Saint Catherine near Arras. I think it was while on a working party but as there are no officers of his company left I am unable to tell you for certain. He has been buried in that district and if you were to write to the "Graves Registration Committee, War Office London" they would probably be able to send you a few more particulars and also a photograph of the grave.

I am very sorry but I am unable to give you further particulars than these.

Yours sincerely
Frederick. J. Standring 2nd Lieut.
"B" Company

8

. . . . A good friend of Frank's, Aitkenhead by name, was killed two days before him & they are both lying near to one another. I feel more sorry for you all than words can tell & I can assure you I miss him very much indeed; for almost two & a half years we were never separate. No doubt you will be wondering why you have never heard from any of the officers in the Coy. but owing to us moving into the trenches about that date & also preparing for the advance on the 9th. things were in a bit of a mix up. None of our officers came back or I can assure you you would have received a letter from them. They all liked Frank

. . . . . We used to talk of the meetings we would have after this war was all over but alas Im the only one left now. I hope your father is bearing up under his great loss & trusting this finds you all in the best of health

I am
Yours very sincerely,
Andrew Hamilton

9

Here in the forest
Our present and our future
Are one with our past

Trompettes des Morts

Diagonal rays filter through branches,
Criss-cross the pathway with neat shadow-lines
That stretch from the trunks like hands on a clock-face
No longer concerned with the passing of time.

Trompettes des Morts push up through the groundswell
The groundswell of flowers with Milk Caps and Morels.
Trompettes des Morts, a strange silent fanfare,
Push up through the ivy with Ceps and Chanterelles.

Someone steps on a twig. The sharp crack breaks open
A door in my mind that was kept locked before.
It lets out a deafening bombardment of music,
It lets out the hideous harmonics of war.

I try not to hear the star-shells, the "Whiz-bangs".
I try not to listen to inhuman screams.
I try not to see bodies shattered by shrapnel
Nor the dead who will rise up and walk through my dreams

But I cannot escape the burden of history.
I reach out to them. They reach out to me
For their flesh fed the rebirth of this mighty forest,
Their blood formed this whispering carpet of leaves.

Time-traveller

I'm a traveller through time, drawn back by a soldier.
His eyes from a photograph silently call.
He lifts long-dead fingers, crooks them and beckons,
"Come back to the Somme, lass, then you will know all."

I stumble through platitudes pencilled on post-cards,
Tiptoe through letters that skirt round the truth,
Wade through a welter of micro-fiche newsprint
Led on by the gaze of a khaki-clad youth.

I'm a traveller through time, and I'm going nowhere.
There's no map of the country where I want to be.
Then a hand clasps my shoulder – I know without looking
The boy in the photo has come to help me ...

I see severed limbs alive with white maggots,
A head with no face is a food-bowl for rats,
And bodies, rough-buried – no crosses or blessings,
Marked only by rifles and battered tin hats.

I stare as a stallion impaled on a poplar
Paws at the air in its gruesome death-dance.
I flinch as men trample on their wounded comrades
While officers order, "Advance, men. Advance."

His voice is as dry as the rustle of paper,
His whisper falls light as a leaf from a tree.
His eyes are dark tunnels, bewildered and haunted,
"I've shown you the truth, lass. Now you must help me.

So tell me, Time-traveller, our lives weren't wasted
For I cannot rest till the day that I find
Proof that our suffering made your world the better.
Can you ease the pain in my unquiet mind?"

Two generations
Crossed mountains of war, to reach
This plateau of peace.

Into the Past …

"Kitchener wants YOU" appealed directly to the men, as did the heroic images of duty, honour and patriotism.

Other posters called upon women – mothers, wives, sweethearts – to encourage their men to enlist.

Even children were used to shame their fathers into volunteering, by making the reluctant consider how they would be regarded if they did not go to "do their bit."

We Need You

Their conscience said "Go!"
For skilled propaganda
Called the young, fit and healthy
To do the "right thing".
Duty and honour
(And public opinion)
Urged them to fight for
Their country and king.

The slogan touched men who were
Trapped on the treadmill
Of dead-end employment –
They thought it would bring
A chance to "get on",
A chance to "be something"
So they signed on to fight for
Their country and king.

"We need you" appealed to
The thousands of jobless.
It gave pride and purpose,
It tapped the deep spring
That welled up within them,
Cried, "Am I worth nothing?"
They thought they were valued
By country and king.

Freewill

Were you swept on a tide
Of stirring words,
Carried by currents
More powerful than you?
Were you thrilled to be thrust
By magnificent waves,
Towards heroic horizons?

Or were you sucked into war?
Shamed into it, thrown
Into the maelstrom
And pulled down spinning –
Drowning in doubts,
Unable to choose
Your own direction?

The Heart of Midlothian

"In October 1914 two additional New Army battalions of The Royal Scots, both closely connected with Edinburgh, were raised. The 15th The Royal Scots, with which the name of Colonel Sir Robert Cranston will ever be honourably associated, consisted of citizens of the capital with a strong leaven of Scots from Manchester; they were known as "Cranston's Battalion." The eloquent zeal and abounding energy of Sir George McCrae led to the establishment of the 16th The Royal Scots. After a recruiting campaign of only thirteen days a force of 1350 men was formed; it was appropriately called "McCrae's Battalion," since its first commander was the one whose enterprise had brought it into being. It comprised men from all classes, students from the training colleges and universities, artizans, clerks, and a phalanx of footballers; in this connection the patriotic lead given by the Heart of Midlothian Football Club will always be remembered with gratitude and satisfaction by the people of Edinburgh."

"The Royal Scots 1914 - 1919" by Major John Ewing.

The following telegrams were received by the "Hearts" team.
From Dr John Smith, Kirkcaldy (a former Scottish Internationalist) –
With friend M'Dowall I say from the bottom of my heart: Good old Hearts! Well played! I am proud to have been at one time a member of your Club. Your players have set an example to others that they must follow, and then the risk of our good old game becoming as a stink in the nostrils of the nation will be swept away.

From Alfred Davis, Esq. Marlowe (one of the English Association's Vice-Presidents) –
Very heartily congratulate your Club on the splendid response made by your players to the "call to arms." I trust the lead your men have given will be followed by the players of England.

In December 1914 the first English Football Battalion was raised in London.

An Appreciation

By Col. Sir George McCrae, D.S.O., The Royal Scots.

In the closing months of 1914 much recrimination was hurled at the world of sport, and they were freely charged with reluctance to do their bit in the great world war. Much of that criticism was ungenerous and unfair, made without the knowledge of what had been done by the individual.

The raising of a new Kitchener Battalion in Edinburgh gave opportunity of showing of what Scotland's footballers were made.The Heart of Midlothian players made generous response to my appeal for recruits, and a whole company was rapidly raised including some players from other teams in Scotland.

The "Heart" Company has earned never-dying fame in a Battalion which embraced some of the finest material that the British army has ever seen. It was a great combination – a Company of students from Edinburgh University and the training colleges, the "Hearts" Company, two Companies of artizans – all welded together by arduous training into a very fine Battalion. The Battalion has given a good account of itself in many a hard-fought engagement, and where danger has been greatest and the shells falling thickest – there has the "Hearts" been – all "Forwards" then. Their losses, like that of the Battalion, have been severe.

But the glory of it shall never fade, and, to those of us who are left, the comradeship and good feeling which pervaded all ranks will ever be a happy recollection.

We are proud of our fallen heroes. They have made the supreme sacrifice willingly, gladly, for a great cause.

Their memory shall be ever green. Their deeds a stimulus to like effort to all who follow in their train."

"The 'Hearts' and the Great War" by John M'Cartney.

Frankie had taken his preliminary Pharmaceutical Examination while employed in A. L. Laing's chemist shop in Lerwick, and subsequently went to Edinburgh to continue his training. He was a keen sportsman, and a staunch "Hearts" supporter. He therefore joined The 16th The Royal Scots (McCrae's Battalion) in October 1914.

The Scott Boys Enlist

Sgt. William Scott.

Pte. Bertram Scott.

Cpl. Thomas M. Scott.

Pte. Samuel H. Scott.

Sgt. Francis H. Scott.

What's the use of troubling?

The following extract (Frankie – 15/3/16) shows that the song "Pack up your troubles" did reflect accurately the fatalistic attitude of the soldiers, at least at the beginning. It refers to the Tribunals set up to consider the cases of those who, for a variety of reasons, wished to be excused from active service. Many of these were Conscientious Objectors who objected to fighting on moral or religious grounds. Frankie clearly had little sympathy with their point of view.

The Tribunal will certainly be busy dealing with all those cases but I don't suppose very many of them will get off. I don't know why any young or eligible man wants to get off unless of course, he's situated something like Alex L. Certainly the life is not all "milk & honey" but it's not so bad as some folks would have you believe. I think the worst of it is the training, for you do get some "hot stuff" to do sometimes. Since coming out here it is much easier, of course there is danger & some risks but you have them in civy life as well, & if you're going to come out safe you're as well here as at home. I think everybody turns "Fatalist" when they come out & believe that if a shot is meant for you, you'll get it, if not, whats the use of troubling.

War Fever

It was the thrill,
The beautiful hate of it
Fired us with frenzy,
With lust for the kill.
Hate made us smile
As we shot human targets,
Hate made us cheer
As we saw their blood spill.

We wanted vengeance
For the Hun "frightfulness".
We heard the pipes
And we rushed to their call ...
We were Death-bringers,
Warriers, Berserkers
Eager to feast
In great Sidfodr's hall.

'Hun frightfulness' was a term used to describe German behaviour which was considered to contravene all laws of decency and fair play, and was popularly understood to be an inherent part of German Kultur.

The sinking of the 'Lusitania' was one example of this. A Cunard liner, she was carrying 2000 civilian passengers. 1198 of them drowned. This was regarded as a moral outrage, and was put to good use by British propaganda to promote war frenzy.

What was not public knowledge was that the ship was carrying arms, and that the captain ignored all six warnings he was given by wireless about enemy submarines in the area, and failed to comply with advice laid down by the admiralty as regards safe passage through a war zone.

The Fury of War

"Another circumstance that gave a peculiar character to the fighting in 1916 was that the fury of the war was then at its zenith,and although individual acts of chivalry were not uncommon, British and Germans regarded each other with a passion and rancour that over-mastered the promptings of pity and mercy. Exhulting like inquisitors at the burning of a heretic, men expressed a barbarous joy at the suffering of their opponents. Some seemed to look on the war as a kind of grotesque art and professed to find a symphonic dignity in a bombardment. Others (extremely few) were addicted to the horrors of war as a degenerate is to a drug: These experienced a holy pleasure …"

"The Royal Scots 1914 - 1918" by Major John Ewing.

While I have no evidence of anything as extreme as this in the brothers, there are many references to their eagerness for action, at least in the early stages.

Tom, writing from Gallipoli (where they were in action against the Turks) makes the following play on words *"I am sorry that I can't send you home a Turk-ey for Christmas, but I don't think we can spare them. We want to salt everyone down we can catch. Lead is splendid salting stuff!"*

Willie wrote to his brother-in-law that he was *"longing to have a go at the beggars …"*

Bertie refers to *"good shooting"*, and Frank wrote that *"Sunday was a great day. The artillery went the whole of the time …"*

Savage Fighting (Tommy 14/8/16)

"The fire was terrible, for the air was literally charged with lead, but our luck was evidently in for after reaching shelter our losses were found to be ridiculously small. I put it down to an act of providence. The Turks seeing us retiring naturally thought we were the whole of the opposing forces, and followed up our retirement falling neatly into the trap prepared for them. They followed right up the gully and when every man had entered, the Infantry, which was being held for the job, closed round behind them, completely cutting them off. Thus ended so many Dusky Abduls; for what were not shot gave themselves up and were taken prisoner."

He wrote about another episode as follows:

Dismounting for action we advanced on foot as far out towards the enemy as possible without being observed and succeeded in getting sufficiently close enough to make rifle shooting pretty sure. We got the order to fix bayonets and lay and waited. We didn't have long to wait until we heard an awfully shouting of "Allah" "Allah" "Allah" from thousands of Turks. They got fairly close then before we opened fire and instead of us being surprised as the Turks thought the tables were turned and for the moment they were checked. They never got close enough for the bayonet as we shot them down as fast as they liked to come. Their numbers were too great to be held back for long by the Light Horse alone, but we stuck to our posts like leeches holding them back for five hours, giving the Scotch Infantry sufficient time to firmly establish themselves in trenches behind which they did remarkably well under a perfect hail of machine gun and shrapnel fire.

He goes on to describe the action of the "Scotch" Infantry, and comments that *"they positively gloried in it."*

24

What did you expect –
Short sharp battles, victory
And home by Christmas?

Preserved Trenches

Beaumont – Hamel

Vimy Ridge

Trench Life

At first the reality of trench life was very different from what they expected – extreme discomfort, long spells of boredom and little opportunity for active fighting. They almost welcomed enemy action as a relief from the tedium of repetitive labour or inactivity – particularly if the shells were "duds", as they often were. Their main enemies were cold (or heat), wet, mud, rats, lice and a diet of bully beef and hard biscuits.

Cold in Northern France (Frankie 27/2/16)

Our chief trouble was trying to keep warm. We had hard frost + snow the whole time so I can tell you it was bitterly cold. It did not seem to matter how much clothes you had on the 'beezer' got in all right. I had on so much that I could hardly get my hand up as far as my head. We had sheep skin coats + gloves issued to us so if it had not been for them I don't know what we should have done. The greatest ordeal of the lot was getting a wash, you had to break ice about an inch + a half thick so I can assure you we did not waste any time about it, washing was done in record time.

Cold in Gallipoli (Tommy 1/12/15)

The Young Men's Christian Association
and the
Australian Branch Red Cross

✚

with

H. M. Mediterranean Expeditionary Force in Egypt.

From Tom
No. 983 Coy, 1 Regiment Batt.
Brigade A. L. H. Divisn Gallipoli

1 Decr. 1915.

Dear Lollie,

Sorry I've been so long in writing, but its been so cold my hands and feet are nearly frozen off. It snowed all night and most of the day and been freezing for the last four days. In the trenches of a night my feet get so cold, they feel as if they would drop off. If you would be so kind as to send me a pair of good warm socks and gloves as soon as ever you get this I would be very much obliged. If you Register it I think it would get here quicker. We have all been issued with a sheep skin waistcoat I tell you it is just the thing I have plenty of underclothing and can keep quite warm if it wasn't for my feet and hands. I never felt the cold so much in all my life. It makes a fellow think of home sweet home. A fellow will be able to appreciate a bit of comfort after this. Everything here is just the same as ever. I dunno how the Turks get on this weather, but they keep on firing away as much as ever, there's always some of them coming in and they look pretty well done up. I think if this weather continues it will play up with a lot of them. I was in the trenches last night ..

28

Palestine
12/7/18

Dear Lillie,

I haven't received a letter from you for weeks & weeks. I got no doubt they must have got "bunched" on the road. We are still down amongst the flies, mosquitoes & dust etc in the Jordan Valley, the heat is something awful. Its getting too hot for the flies even, the thunthing a good few of the boys out in the flags, a few pinni, or few away every day, with "malarias." Its subufod so hot, and feel as fit as a fiddle, but th' heather not now too keen. We are getting the flags, as the flags, in no short of mares. I have been on no end of duty every night guard or other duty every night

---

(bar an) for the last fortnight, so there are only about three app. & la. for duty in the Squadron. I am minding the while on water guard. I am comfort under a big tree and the wadi, (hum) I still you under call it at home) night alongside side as I can tell you I'm making the most of it, as we are hardly any within a mile or so of the water, having a bath every now or then and trying to drink as much water as I can to make up for all the times I've gone thirsty. A fellow feels thirsty nearly all the time in this country, and water is generally pretty dear. I suffers its owning to the heat. I had a great ride the night before last. I was detailed to take charge of eighteen camels.

Shells, heat and singing … (Frankie 15/3/16)

Sunday was a great day, the artillery went the whole time, but as far as I could see did very little damage. There was one shell landed quite near us but it was 'dud' & never exploded. They send over quite a lot of these "duds" & one afternoon I counted ten in about an hour. We had splendid weather, just like summer, especially the last two days it was so very warm that we nearly all got a touch of sunburn. It's funny weather for the last time in we could do nothing for the cold & this time we could do less for the heat. We were very cosy in our dug-out, the whole place was covered in & we all had a limited space to curl up in so when we got the brazier going we could sleep as well as if we were in feather beds & imagine we were all safely at home, I'll admit it took some imagination. At nights when we were all in & work finished we used to have well sing songs "in moderato" & to hear us you would have thought the Huns were miles away instead of yards.

The Conscientious Exhilarator

"Every encouragement should be given for singing and whistling."—(Extract from a "Military Manual.")

That painstaking fellow, Lieut. Orpheus, does his best, but finds it uphill work at times

The chances are that Lt. Orpheus is whistling 'It's a long way to Tipperary'. It was the hit song of the war. Composed by a market stall holder, Jack Judge, it was taken up by the Germans as well as the Allies — much as Lili.

Marlene was popular on both sides in WW2. The French and the Belgians often used it as an alternative to God Save the King, as the British National Anthem.

"Going in" and "Coming out" (Frankie 29/11/16)

Well, Roldie, there's really nothing much going on here just the usual routine, in & out of trenches & sometimes I wonder which is the worse. Certainly the worst part of it is the going in & the coming out; so The pack we have to carry is no joke, some of items are greatcoat, furry coat, Waterproof cape & sheet. besides a change of underclothing & a few odds & ends & then we have gas helmets hung over us & what with one thing & another every man is loaden up like a pack mule. You might see if Ganson does'nt have an old cart he could lend me, I might be able to get all the stuff in it.

Ganson Brothers were originally pony carriage hirers, with stables at Market Street and Harbour Street, Lerwick. Later they ran a car hire and bus service.

And a Few Other Things

Napoleon said: "Every soldier carries a field marshal's bâton in his knapsack"

The soldier went into battle carrying an extraordinary range of equipment about his person — a sample mix might be two blankets, groundsheet, spare coat, spare boots, shovel, mess tins, 150 rounds of ammunition, rifle, bayonet, water bottle, towel and many smaller items. The French soldier also carried a couple of litres of wine, hand grenades and gas masks and while the equipment load of the British was about 65 lbs, the Frenchman's was nearer 85 lbs and the German's would sometimes exceed even that figure.

33

Weather and rats (Frankie 8/10/16)

> . . . . Of course the winter is coming in now & with it the usual mess up of mud & water but then that's just what to expect, & keep in mind that there's a war on. In fact our worst enemies are the weather & the rats. I thought I knew what rats were but find out now that I knew absolutely nothing about them. We have got quite accustomed to them so don't mind them much except when the beggars start eating our rations & then of course we strongly object & let them know of our objections with the aid of a hefty stick. We are doing rather lon...

Spells in the Trenches

> . . . . We are doing rather longer spells in the trenches now than formerly. Our usual is about sixteen days doing the reserve, support & front line, in that time & then have four or five days out, but everything is much better now in the way of accommodation & we always have good dug-outs so are fairly comfortable. Just now we are in the dugouts

Frankie 5/11/16

This old country is about six times as cold as you are at home, especially when you are over the bootheads in mud and doing patrols nearly all night. However it's all in a life time and I consider that we are jolly lucky to be here at all … our last two or three days in (the line) were très bon. We were in reserve and I had a fine dugout which I improved by doing a bit of a wander and finding an old sandbag bed and a brazier, collared both and began making myself comfortable. You know, after ten months of trenches you begin to know what's what and can take care of yourself.

Trench diagram

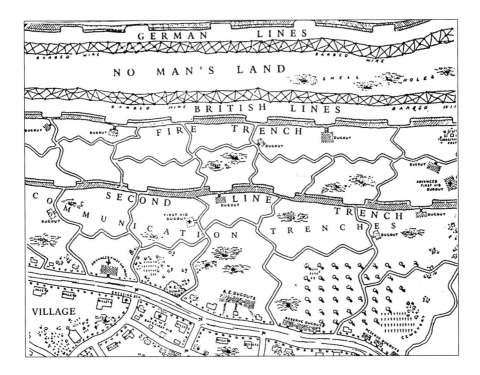

This diagram shows the three-tier system of reserve, support and front line. They were linked by a network of communication trenches, and interspersed with dugouts and First Aid Posts. The zig-zags were designed to contain the blast of exploding shells, and limit their effect. In busy battle zones the whole area was cratered with shell-holes, and the lines practically ceased to exist.

War news

Both Tommy and Frankie asked for information as to how the war was progressing, as they knew only about their own sector. Frankie wrote on 15/3/16: *"Did I tell you your letters are not censored? So you might give me some news as to what is going on, for of course we just get scraps of news here and there."* On 29/11/16 he wrote:

> . . . . . . I was very pleased to get all that information regarding the reserves etc of the Hun. Of course, you know that we don't have much idea of what's going on except at our own particular bit of the line so it was all the more welcome. . . . .

Their letters were of course censored. Tommy (27/5/16) writes from the Sinai Peninsula:

> . . . . . . I am sorry I can't give you any information as regards the positions we are holding here, as the letters have to pass the censor, but we are in the first line of defence and might have a slap at the Turks anytime.

The Battle of the Somme

Prior to the attack there was a week-long bombardment which culminated in the detonation of a series of mines. This was intended to destroy the barbed wire, enemy artillery, trenches, fortified villages (such as La Boisselle) and machine-gun posts. The men were told it would be "a walk-over", and that they would meet with little or no resistance.

The truth was rather different. The bombardment was ineffective due to the poor quality of British shells. Many were "duds" with faulty fuses. There were far too few of them, and they were unsuited to the task. In addition to this, the German dugouts beneath the trenches and the villages were so deep and so strongly built that they withstood the shelling. The result was that when the bombardment ceased the German soldiers emerged unharmed, and the British troops were mown down by machine-guns they believed to be destroyed.

There were, of course, other factors involved. The following extract comes from "Never Such Innocence" by Martin Stephen:

"Generals were sometimes hated by their men, but more hatred seems to have been directed at staff-officers, for the age-old reason that they were not fighting, but were giving the orders to men who were. It must be remembered that a majority of officers in the front line believed, as did Haig, that the barrage would cut the wire, and that the Germans would be pounded to dust in their trenches. The stories whereby officers in trenches pleaded with higher authority to be allowed to change the main battle plan to adapt to local conditions have become part of the folk-myth. …Such stories are used to illustrate the idiocy of higher command, and the wholly unthinking manner in which offensives were planned and executed. The problem with this view is that it is too simple …"

Stephen points out that several other factors should also be taken into account, such as the "huge size of the army", problems of communication, and the inexperience and limited training of the New Army Battalions. He concludes "that does not excuse the carnage of the Somme, but it helps to explain why it happened".

Lochnagar Crater

Lochnagar was the name given to one of the sixteen mines which were blown along the enemy lines at 7:28a.m. on July 1, 1916. Cecil Lewis (who served with the Royal Flying Corps) describes in his book "Sagittarius Rising" how he watched the opening attack from his plane above Thiepval.

"At Boisselle the earth heaved and flashed. There was an ear-splitting roar, drowning all the guns, flinging the machine sideways in the repercussing air. The earthy column rose, higher and higher to almost four thousand feet."

60,000 lbs of ammonal were used, brought through a network of tunnels from the Tara-Usna line. The explosion left a crater 300 feet across and 90 feet deep.

Lochnagar

I stand by the crater – nauseous, light-headed
(EVITER D'ENTRER, EROSION SEVERE).
I see little pathways, little chalk pathways
Trickle in frozen streams down to the depths.

They point to white crosses and faded red flowers.
This vast concave emptiness holds only death.
"The blast burst our eardrums. I can't describe it,"
He wrote. "I've no words for that volume of noise,

But that was the signal, the two-minute signal
To march to the trenches we thought were destroyed.
Oh, you'd have been proud of us, every last one of us,
The Sixteenth, the Royals Sir George McCrae's boys,

For into the hellfire of bullets and shellfire
The Heart of Midlothian went over the top.
Out into No-Man's-Land, we followed orders
(If you aren't dead, men, it's treason to stop)."

Now modern-day farmers use combines and tractors
To cut down and harvest a different green crop.

The Great Push (Frankie 16/7/16)

18907.

'a' Company

16th July.

16th Bn. Royal Scots,

B. E. F.   France

My Dear Rollie,

Very many thanks for
yours which I received yesterday, it
having taken over a week to come.
but I suppose things will be a bit
upset just now. I hope you have
received my post-cards all right
letting you know I was still alive
+kicking. I am sorry I have not
managed to write sooner but have
been kept pretty busy lately. I
was very sorry to hear that you
were not in the best of health
but hope your holiday has turned
out a success, +that you are feeling
much the better of it.

Well, Rollie, I suppose you will
be wondering how I got on in the
"great push". I wrote Daddy a
short note but I suppose you would

The Great Push (Continued)

not see it as you were not at home, so I will try & give you a slight idea of what happened where we were. Of course you would know of the great bombardment which was going on along the line & I can assure you our sector was not missed. This bombardment kept going for seven days & then we got orders to move up the line & get ready. We were up & took up our positions when the bombardment started at about twenty times as strong ever & kept on for an hour & a half. What a row! you can have no idea of it, nobody could hear another speak for the noise, this was from about 6.a.m to 7.30 am on the memorable 1st. At about 7.15 the mines started to go up shaking the whole ground. I thought the whole earth was going to open & swallow the lot of us. Then at

41

7.30 a.m the order came to "get over." We were at a part of the line where the trenches were about 500 yds apart so had a good bit of ground to cover before reaching the enemy's front line, & that, no mans land, was where we had most of our causualities. It was a pure Hell, crossing that ground, owing to their machine guns to hell fire. It was awful seeing all your chums go under & not being able to do anything for them. However some of us managed to get over. all right & found their front line absolutely battered to bits, practically just chalk heaps etc. & hardly anybody in it. Those left were so demoralised that they hadn't a fight left in them but surrended right away. They came running forward with their hands up & shouting "Kamarad". after taking this line we went on & took the second & then the third line which we consolidated + occupied. We had some fighting to do to take these but our boys never stopped but took everything before them but I can tell you it was chronic work. We found that man to man we could beat them every time but those working guns of theirs made cruel work of us. Naturally our causualities were very heavy but fortunately they were chiefly wounded + most of them slight at that. The percentage of killed was comparatively small. Our platoon seemed to catch it extra hot for out of 40 of us who went over only six of came out unhurt. Heaven only knows how I managed to come through but I had some narrow shaves. There are five different shots through different parts of my equipment + I had a shot which just grazed my neck but did not break the skin, so I have a lot to be thankful for. We held on to our position for three days before we were relieved & these three days were about the worst I've ever had. We were out on bombing raids etc. two or three times a day & hardly got a minutes sleep the whole time. Our grub consisted of two or three hard biscuits until the third day when our ration party managed to get up, & I don't think I ever saw a more welcome set of chaps as they were. We were sort of water also so altogether, to put it in Army language, it was an absolute b . However all things come to an end & so did our torture. We were relieved on the Tuesday & have been back here resting since. We are about five miles off the original line & although the camp in not anything great it is a haven compared to what we have come through.

Chain of Command

Smart politicians
With hidden agendas sent
Memos to Gen'rals

Gen'rals in war-rooms
Played games with toy soldiers, sent
Orders to Red Tabs

Red Tabs in chateaux
Sent ill-founded directives
To men at front lines

Reluctant Lieutenants
Led trusting young soldiers
To meet certain death

MPs betrayed them
From a safe distance, without
Soiling their hands

Moodswing

First indignation
As "poor little Belgium"
Tried to stand up
To the Prussian Goliath.

Then came propaganda
And Kitchener's poster
With its Pointing Finger –
The recruitment drive.

Then there was outrage
When they sank "Lusitania"
With the loss of twelve hundred
Civilian lives.

Outrage was transformed.
Became need-to-take-action,
For-King-and-country
And national pride.

Pride became duty,
Enlistment and training.
"Kill, kill and kill.
Don't leave one Bosche alive."

Hate died at the Somme
Became disillusion
For they used men like pawns
In a game based on lies.

Word on field post-cards
Shielded loved ones from the truth
Read between the lines

A Bushel of Silence

The average soldier … suffers, and he buries his suffering under a bushel of silence, admitting only that this was "pretty rotten", or that was "pretty hot while it lasted."
Robert M. Greig (Shetland Times reporter – 1920)

Frankie's letters use the same kind of understatement.

Yes, this part of the line is a bit busier than it used to be in the way of shelling etc., but so far I have always been lucky. The shells are not so bad but these Minnaewefers of his are the boys. They come over "shü-ing" like an express train + don't forget to leave a mark where they land, however we can generally hear them coming + get a few seconds to get out of the way.

. I see you think you would be quaking with fear if shelled, well I can't say I felt 'fear' exactly, but it was more a feeling of "awe" that came over me as naturally you are pretty helpless + can't do anything while these things are coming over.

Comforts for the Troops

Spirits were buoyed up by the cameraderie between the men, whose loyalties now lay more with their Unit than with King and Country. They were bonded by their experiences at the Somme, and criticised (among themselves) the wisdom of their orders and those who gave them. They showed a determination to find humour in every grim situation, or to trivialise it. This to some extent defused the danger, misery and horror they were immersed in.

Martin Stephen, in "Never Such Innocence", describes humour as "a form of exorcism". Undoubtedly this was so. Frontline newspapers such as "Wipers Times" were full of humorous articles, comic poems and parodies, jokes and cartoons.

Songs of all kinds were sung. Stephen notes that "To be successful a song needed a number of features. It had to be strongly rhythmic and simple because the songs were sung most often … when marching. A good song was either thoroughly obscene or grossly sentimental, wholly unconcerned with the wider issues of life and the war, and frequently mocking about the army and its personalities. Above all the songs were basic – basic about life, about sexuality, and about death … The soldiers in their songs are in their own way expressing something so basic and simple that it slips through the fingers of the great poets."

Civilians took up collections to send "comforts for the troops", and gathered sphagnum moss to dress their wounds.

Soldiers looked forward to the wine, women and song of garrison towns; and to visiting "estaminets" in villages near rest camps. Even illness was welcomed as it could mean a spell in a hospital bed, away from the trenches. A "Blighty One" was best – a wound so severe it meant being sent back to England, and days were counted to elusive home leave.

Letters from home were eagerly anticipated, as were parcels of gloves, socks, chocolate, cocoa, magazines and cigarettes …

My grandfather must have spent countless hours writing to his brothers, striving to strike the right note which would offer comfort, understanding, information, love, encouragement – and reassurance that a "normal" world still existed away from the chaos and carnage they had to endure; and to, somehow, lift their spirits for a moment. It must have been a lonely and heart-rending task.

Dear Brother,

Here by the hearth, when Kathie's asleep,
I shed my cheerful daytime mask,
And search my aching heart for words
To write to you – a troubling task ...

I stir the embers, sit and stare
At images appearing there.
Men choke and drown in dying coals –
Now stinking, ordure-filled shell-holes.
You've never told me, but I find
Your wordless truths fly mind to mind.
Mangled bodies, tangled wire –
Hideous pictures in the fire.

Your letters carefully conceal
The depth of suffering that you feel.
Unspoken rules say, "Hide your tears,
Don't tell the facts, don't name your fears
To acknowledge makes them so,
Play the ostrich, they may go.
Each of us must spare the other.
Brother must give strength to brother."

I write, therefore, of trivial things,
Keep the tone light-hearted, bring
A touch of humour here and there,
A smile to counteract despair ...
I strive to generate a view
Of "normal", humdrum life for you,
Of sanity – an anchor for
You to hold through this mad war.

I never show the pain I keep
Locked inside, nor how I weep
As kneeling down I plead and pray,
"God, spare my brothers one more day."
My helplessness is hard to bear
When Death walks at your shoulder there.
We must not rail against His will.
He tests us hard, but loves us still ...

I'll stand a moment by the door
To clear my throbbing head before
I climb the weary, creaking stairs –
But dark thoughts catch me unawares.
While I watch flickering Northern Lights,
Gunfire's aurora fills your nights,
Its hideous beauty silhouettes
Those who guard the parapets.

Your suffering torments my mind's eye
With brutish fantasies, and I
Can only write, and send you love ...
With cigarettes and socks and gloves.

Letter from Lerwick

Vingolf.
Lerwick . 10 June 1918.

My dear Tommy.

Your nice long interesting letter arrived
per last steamer, and we were pleased to hear of
all your doings against the Turks. You seem
to be too much for them every time. You must
have had a rough time of it living on bully
beef & biscuits in such a hot wilderness for
such a long time. However, we have just
heard from Annie that you are now in Cairo
having a well earned holiday, so we hope you
had a good time to make up for all your privations.
It does seem queer to us to hear of you roaming
round the holy land, living on bully beef and
biscuits; its something like the children of
Israel getting fed up on Manna, in days of old.
You'll be quite an expert in Bible history when
you come home, and the ministers will need
to watch themselves. Sammy arrived home
on draft leave last night. He is looking a.1.
The training has fairly made a man of him.
He says his captain is wanting him to apply
for a Commission, and he may do so. If he
does, he wont go to the front meantime.
He will see about it when he gets back to

2.

England. Bertie is still in hospital getting on slowly. He has been there 6 weeks now, & expects to be another month. In addition to his shin bone being broken, is leg is badly wounded, & the ligaments broken, so it will be some time before he will have the use of his foot, but the Dr. says it will get all right in time. He is quite bright & cheery, & prefers hospital to France, which is very unhealthy in the meantime. Willie is still in charge of the officers mess down in Wiltshire. He is marked for home service for the next six months. He was down at Arbroath last week helping Annie to flit. We are expecting Bobbie will soon be reaching this country again on his Transport. I don't know whether Donnie is coming back or not. He wasn't sure when he left this country. Jimmy is up in Queensland at present beside Uncle Peter. He always seems to be in a swither whether to stick to the sea or go in for farming.

Mackie & I are still civilians, & Peter is still on the Pharos. You would have heard that Annie got a little girl recently & so did Peter, & of course you know of my one. He is doing splendidly. In fact all the additional scotts are getting on first rah. You'll have quite a number

Letter from Lerwick (Continued)

of nephews & neices to inspect when you come home.
I dont know what news I've told you about the
boys at the front. I think I told you that B.
Kay & George Tulloch were killed. George Burgess
is a prisoner in Germany. Tommy White and
Freddy Leask are missing. I'm afraid they are
both killed, as it is a long time now since
they went amissing & nothing has been heard of
them since. They were in the front line when
the big German attack began in the end of March.
There is a good bit of stir on here again one way
and another. The Shetland folk saw an
Aeroplane for the first time last week. She
went snoring over Lerwick & gluffed the wits
out of all the old women. There's a lot of
football going on between the different branches
of the service, but there is no Lerwick team
now. The boys have all been called up,
and there's nobody left to play —
Very little golf is being played now. Over 50 of
our members are in A.M.Forces, & there are no
competitions being held. I have a game now
and again but we cant get to Bressay for
want of Petrol. The launches dont run now.
Mackie & I & Bonnie Irvine were at the haddocks
on Wednesday. We had a long line with us, and
had a great time pulling away "oot be sooth"

to get her set. It was a stiff breeze of south wind, and we nearly pulled our arms out of the sockets getting to the fishing grounds. At last we got the line set, and started fishing with handlines until the fish had time to get on the big line. Then we discovered we had set the bally line on a minefield, and two mine-sweepers came out & swept away out 'outermost bough' & broke 'da burroo', so we had to let go everything & rescue 'da bough'. After that we 'hailed' the line and got almost the fill of a herring basket. all whitings & haddocks, except one peerie crooner which had lost its way & swallowed one of our hooks in error. When we got everything clued up, we hailed Lowrie Leask who was passing in a sailing boat, & he came up alongside & took our painter, & towed us safely to Hay's Dock, where we landed our catch at 11 p.m. after a strenuous nights work. We then shared out the fish and I lugged my share home, and we've been living on sookit fish ever since. We're on meat rations now, so the fish comes in very handy. We get barely ¾ lb of meat per week, and ½ lb of ham or bacon, so we have to be careful we don't eat it all up the first day of the week. The kids only get half rations. We get 2 ozs tea, 5 ozs butter, + ½ lb sugar per week, but in the meantime

Letter from Lerwick (Continued)

bread & oatmeal is not rationed, so we are all right. The above is the rations for each person. The boat was late this week & we could get no meat for Sunday, so we had sookit whitings for our Sunday dinner. I'm seen da day at we wid a turned up wir nose at a sookit whiting, bit heth wir blyde to get dem noo.

Well Tom, I dont think I have any more news this time, I wrote you a short time ago. We are all very well. Kathleen is wearing the necklace you sent her & is very proud of it. She will soon be getting her school holidays, & then the whole family is going to Braewick.

Kathie sends her love to you, & Kathleen sends × × × × × ×.

Your aff brother

Lollie.

Write soon again.

This is the only example of the many letters he wrote. Although it was written on 10th June, Tommy had not received it when he wrote his last letter home on 12th July (see page 93), and it was returned with his effects – unopened.

L. G. Scott – a portrait of my grandfather.

Laurence Gray Scott was born in Lerwick in 1879. He left school at thirteen and went to work as "general dog's-body" in the Sheriff Clerk's Office, Lerwick.

He was ambitious, and taught himself shorthand in order to become a clerk. After a year or so he went to work in Edinburgh to "better himself", but returned when he was twenty, seriously ill with T.B.. He was not expected to live. He was advised to get plenty of fresh air and gentle exercise. His father bought him a rowing boat, and he enjoyed "aandooin" in the harbour, or across to Bressay. His attitude was very positive. He cycled a lot, and took regular daily walks round the town. This was when he became friendly with the blind scholar J. J. Haldane Burgess who influenced his thinking, and helped him map out his "reading programme". He read avidly and widely all his life, and always had a list that he worked through methodically.

When his health improved, he took a job as clerk in R. and C. Robertson (Licenced Grocer) Lerwick, then at Anderson and Co. He soon became manager; and, after the war, partner (junior then senior).

He was a very good photographer, a keen gardener and a faithful church worker, but his main interests were geology and archaeology. During my childhood my family went with him on regular outings throughout the summer. The object was to survey a particular area and take measurements (and other details) of 'picts' houses" which he'd found. We children regarded it as a privilege to hold the tape measure! He passed on his findings to C. T. S. Calder of the Royal Commission of Ancient Monuments, Scotland – and for this he was made a Fellow of the Society of Archaeologists, Scotland. These trips taught us the geography of Shetland, and gave many opportunities to learn about its flora and fauna. His love of these islands was highly infectious!

As a young man he was secretary to the Brass band, the Templar's Football Club, Lerwick Regatta Committee, Cycling Club and others besides! He wrote humorous songs and skits for concerts. Later he wrote dialect stories and articles for the "New Shetlander" magazine. No wonder his brother Donnie said he envied him his "headgear" i.e. brainpower!

Above all he was a family man. He and my grandmother were a devoted couple. My mother adored him, and they shared many interests. He told her a great deal of family history, which she passed on to me. During my teenage years I spent many hours with him and my grandmother. Sometimes we read quietly together, while he smoked his pipe. Sometimes Granny and I sewed while we talked – often about their (very different) childhoods, or what we would now call "local studies". I never saw him ruffled. He was always calm, loving, supportive, informative, interested in everything, and full of stories and laughter.

I admired him and I loved him dearly. What more can I say?

Delville Wood (Devil's Wood) 1916 and 2000

Devil's Wood

"Princes Street" they called it,
That trench through Bois d'Elville,
A thoroughfare congested –
But not with the genteel
Tip-tapping feet of shoppers,
Auld Reekie's well-shod wives –
But the weary mud-clogged traffic
Of the men who dealt in lives.

Today we walk in silence
Through that same "Princes Street",
Tall trees all around us,
Smooth turf beneath our feet ...

But the silence in the forest
Is an uneasy thing.
I find no solace in this place
Where no bird dares to sing
Except an unseen cuckoo
Whose two-note melody
Speaks for the lost, untimely-dead.
It says, "Remember me."

True Colours

Take the red of wild poppies,
Of fire and of blood;
The brown of the rats
And the deep Flanders mud;
The green (once the colour
Of lush meadow grasses)
That now marks the path
Of the poisonous gases.

Add the yellow of song-birds
(The tunnelers' warning)
And the grey of the mist
In the cold light of morning
When the shell-shocked were marched out,
Blindfolded and shot
As cowards and traitors –
Guilty or not ...

Now blend in the blue
Of the Picardy sky
That witnessed the slaughter
That First of July.
Mix this painful palette
And you will create
The colour of darkness,
Of war and of hate.

Gas

Chlorine Gas was first used by the Germans in April 1915. It was released from cylinders and formed a sinister greenish cloud which rolled along the ground. The effects were ghastly – vomiting, choking and death (if it was inhaled in large enough quantities). Everything it touched was stained green, even human skin. The British began to manufacture it the following month.

Other types of gas were used later. Scientists worked to produce toxic gases which were more lethal and more controllable. Phosgene left men drowning in fluid produced by their own lungs; and mustard gas blistered the skin (even through clothing), blinded them (temporarily), and killed if inhaled.

Cylinders were soon replaced by shells which could place the poison more accurately, and both sides produced more efficient types of gas masks.

Shot at Dawn

Three hundred and six men were shot as traitors or cowards during the First War. Many were confused by the smoke, noise … and the sudden disappearance of men who were at one moment standing beside them, and the next blown away by a shell. Many were concussed by the explosions. And, yes, some did run away, particularly from toxic gas. Many are now believed to have been suffering from shell-shock, a blanket term for all forms of post-traumatic stress. However, fearing indiscipline and mutiny, those in command were ruthless in dealing with such incidents. The men were tried. Such defence as was presented was largely ignored. Many were convicted and sentenced to death often on the flimsiest of evidence, and faced a firing squad made up of their own comrades. Their deaths were to be a deterrent to others.

These executions remain a very sensitive issue. Descendants of the victims mounted a campaign in 1995 seeking pardons for their soldier-ancestors. In 1998 they were allowed to lay wreaths at the cenotaph, but that is as far as the present government is prepared to go to date. Obviously a certain percentage of these cases were guilty of deserting their posts deliberately; and, although many of these "top secret" files have been opened, it is well-nigh impossible to ascertain all the facts surrounding individual cases. It is a case of "guilty till proven innocent". The whole matter is shrouded in doubt, guilt and incredible sadness.

From the Trenches

Beneath my feet dead soldiers groan,
Shout their curses, sigh and moan,
Laugh too loud, or softly drone
Their prayers in mumbled monotone.

This elegy of echoes flows
And, flower-like, it swells and grows.
Whispers spread out tendril-roots,
Feeble threads become strong shoots

That rise to pierce the thin veneer
Of reverence with their sharp green spears.
These leafless blades wound with their slow
Inexorable crescendo ...

The blackened bud now bursts and shows
The petals of a foetid rose.
The ugly blossom is Despair,
Its sombre music fills the air.

There are no soothing phrases here,
But, after eighty pent-up years,
Only the shrill, sharp voice of fear
Borne on a flood of angry tears.

School Trip

Clutching their clip-boards, they pour down the car-park –
A river of kids slurping Coke, chewing gum.
Snaking through trenches they charge at the double.
"Walk!" calls their teacher. See how they run!

"Keep to the paths" (he must restore order),
Puffing, perspiring – "Come here everyone!"
"Stuff that!" they laugh as they jump on the firestep,
Priming their Mills Bombs and loading their guns.

Over the parapet with their Lee Enfields,
Lobbing grenades (grotesque sound effects).
Then clutching their chests they fall into shell-holes
Groaning and feigning theatrical death.

"Look at those kids," says the party of old folks.
"Someone should teach them to show some respect.
They should not make light of the death of our heroes.
What has the world come to?" Their teacher reflects,

They clown to conceal their burden of sadness.
They're closer than we to the young boys who died,
For most of the soldiers who fell weren't heroes –
Just fun-loving kids with expendable lives.

Back in the class we'll discuss pride and sorrow,
We'll interview old men who fought and survived ...
"Which lasts the longest – the glory or sadness?"
We'll ask centenarians with blind, tear-filled eyes.

Home Leave

This is an extract from a letter written to my grandfather by his brother-in-law, Robert Tulloch (Annie's husband) after Frankie had spent his (only) home-leave with them in Arbroath in February 1917. He did not have enough time to come to Shetland.

"I was awfully sorry you could not have the pleasure of seeing Frank. Do you know he is the only soldier I have ever seen who has been on active service for some time, and who does not show some trace in his appearance of the strain and anxiety of life in trenches. Most fellows I have spoken to have a tired and haunted look in their eyes, some very much so, and every one seems to be sick of it, and has a horror of going back. Frank seemed as if he had come from a tour round the world. He looked the picture of health and had put on 16lbs in weight since he landed in France. He is as tall as I am now and bigger all over and in the best of spirits. Really he was irrepressible, and instead of a war worn veteran we met a gay and laughing young soldier, and we had a most happy time together.

I asked him how he could feel so light-hearted after all he had been through, and he said that while he was awfully cut up about the beginning of last July – losing all his old friends in dozens, and facing ordeals in different ways – he had now come to the stage where everything comes as a matter of course. He was telling us one night about being buried through the explosion of a Jack Johnson shell near him, and only his head was left above old mother earth. In about ten minutes they had him out, but he seemed to regard the whole thing as a very ordinary occurence. Another foot of earth and it would have been all up a tree, but Frank didn't worry about might-have-beens.

To tell you some of the more serious discussions we had, and some of his experiences would occupy too much time and I'm not good at descriptive writing. One thing I can truthfully say, and that is, he has had the luck of the "old boy" himself and it is really marvellous that he is alive to tell the tale. Another virtue of Frank's is that he possesses the modesty in a great degree, so characteristic of all his family, and one can depend on his yarns being unvarnished and uncoloured, and if anything underdone.

I might tell you one incident that occurred on 1st July. He and six others after the objectives had been reached, following the advance, had some prisoners to dispose of. The sergeant in charge (Frank was a corporal at that time) told him to take the prisoners back to the base. He set out and on the way down found another batch going down in charge of another non-com. He therefore handed over his lot to this chap and went back to join his party. When he got there they weren't to be found, and not one has been seen or heard of since. There is nothing but surmise about their fate, but Frank's luck was in that day, and he was well out of it …

It's a rotten business all through, not war but murder, and Germany will have a lot to account for when the bill is made up. I hope and trust that all the boys will be as lucky as Frank and that they will all get safely through it …"

Changing Attitude

The few letters that Frankie wrote after he returned to France show a marked change in his attitude. He is unsettled and clearly now experiences the "horror of going back" which was not apparent when he was on leave.
These extracts of 8/2/17 show how he intends to deal with this.

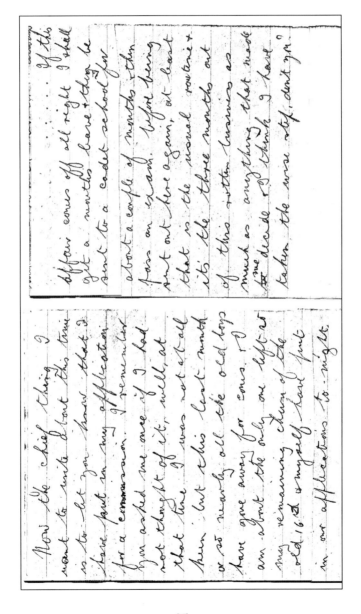

"An Awful Rumour …" (Frankie's last letter 5/3/17)

5/3/17 B.E.F.
France

My Dear Nellie,

Very many thanks for both your letters which I have received all right. I would have written sooner but I was waiting to get this bazaar business settled before I wrote. However everything was postponed owing to our going on the trek. I have been up before the C.O. then the B.O.E. this week-end & got on quite all right I am only waiting now for the return of the papers,

I heard an awful rumour yesterday that the men went to go to Blighty for ... but I hope it is only a rumour. Anyway it

3

will always be a rest, even if I do have to train in France. Of course I don't go into the trenches again as that's always something, at least all the other fellows remained behind the line after ... unconcerned by the B.O.C. so I expect the same will apply to me.

The Book of Remembrance

What could I write
In the Book of Remembrance
But his name and my name
And "Thinking of you"?

A tear, unexpected, fell
Blurring the message
Meant for the grand-uncle
I never knew.

Bertie's Christmas Letter (1917)

191

...think this is the most miserable Christmas I have ever put in as it is snowing and freezing and us poor beggars can't even have a fire on and Christmas without a fire is a blank. There was only one good thing we had plenty to eat and we had three lots of rum to keep the home fires burning in our bellies. I got a parcel from Annie on Christmas eve with a nice big pudding and cake, chocolate and sweets and Ellen little donations and so there

191

are only three of us in this little Regiment we had a good feed I found the threepenny bit in the pudding also the button and the YMCA gave me this little something had each so that was still something to let my Honour it was Christmas. I suppose you will be seeing Willie again soon as he will be getting two rich furlough. I do not know where to send them to so if you would think for me hung for the photos for me would be very much obliged

In the Field,

5 1917

I hope you can read this but the paper is very rough and the pencil I have can't get on much long I have no table and there wait too much light here. Well I don't know much more I can write about. I am quite well but nothing I could get trench fever ___ something to get back to England again. I wish the war would soon end and I am getting quite about full up of it. I had a narrow squeak on Christmas Eve a machine gun

In the Field,

6 191

bullet hit me right on the top of the tin hat but by a good job it glanced off the only damage it did was to dent a little dend in the helmet but a miss is as good as a mile. Well have to stop now hope you are all well Kindest love to all

Your affec Boy

Bertie

Battle of Strazeele (Bertie)

Bertie wrote this account of the Battle of Strazeele in which the Australians blocked the German effort to take the railway centres of Hazebrouck and Caestre. It was here he received the wound which led to his death:

"... then orders came along that we were to stand by ready to move and at seven o'clock that night we marched into Amiens. When we got to the station he was shelling and bombing it so we all had to clear and we had about 20 or 30 casualties there.

He knocked off shelling about midnight and we got back and entrained again bound back to where we had come from. We got to Hazebrouck about two o'clock next afternoon, got off the train and started to march up to the front. He was shelling all the roads so we had to leave them and take an overland route, our destination being to get to Strazeele before Fritz.

Well after jumping ditches and wading through marshes we got there and started digging a line of outposts and by daylight we had a pretty good line formed. Well we were all dog tired and going to have a snooze when orders came that we were not in the right position and that we had to move away, the 3rd Battalion of I. A. relieving us ... and we had to march rightaway round to about the middle of the forest of Nieppe where we had to start to establish ourselves all over again.

We had just got dug in again in front of the forest when orders came for B-Company to move back into the wood and form a support line and of course we had to do it, but I think very little work was done that afternoon. We all laid down anyhow and went to sleep not having had a wink or a feed since we left Amiens.

Well we got back to work about 3 in the morning and got a few posts dug when Fritz started shelling and coming over at us. We kept him back and he never got near us till 10 o'clock when I got hit ... and by the papers he never advanced any that day on us.

By jove you should have seen the cheek of him. He pulled a battery of 77cm field guns into a field about 800 yds away and started banging away. We had great shooting, sniping at them. There were heaps of dead and wounded Germans lying in front of us. I never saw such slaughter in all my life. We had a good many casualties but not a quarter what he had ..."

Vieux – Berquin

Although I found no reference to the Battle of Strazeele in any of the British histories which I have read, it is described in "Guide to Australian Battlefields of the Western Front" by John Laffin. He does not call it by the same name, but it is clearly the same event.

"NIEPPE FOREST ... During the German push of April-May 1918 the 2nd Brigade dug in along the eastern edge, only a kilometre from the village of Vieux-Berquin. The support line was in the forest itself ...

VIEUX-BERQUIN ... This village, between Strazeele and Neuf-Berquin, entered Australian history during the German attempt to break through to the Channel ports in April 1918. What the 7th and 8th Battalions achieved through their steadfast courage greatly helped to stem the enemy push. A plaque on the street wall of the town hall commemorates the feat of arms. The action began on 12 April when the 7th Battalion had been rushed up from the Somme to steady the collapsing British line in Flanders, and actually held by itself about 9 kilometres of vitally important front ... When other 1st Division battalions moved into position, the 7th and 8th Battalions with a combined strength of about 1000 men, held a front of 14 kilometres, a distance which normally would have been held by two divisions. It was a remarkable performance."

The wording on the plaque in Vieux-Berquin ends, "The sister battalions linked in the joint resistance which so materially contributed to the saving of the Channel ports."

Bertie's Wound

This letter was written about 20th April, 1918. It begins,

but the writing deteriorates. He goes on, *"Well I am getting on first rate. It was a piece of high explosive shell that got me. It hit me fair in the shin, about six inches above the ankle, went right through the bone and stopped in the calf of my leg. The piece was taken out and I have got it so I will be able to show it you when I get home. It means lying on the broad of my back for 6 or 8 weeks but the time will soon pass ..."*

He asks my grandfather to send him £1 as he has no money, *"and I will die if I don't get a smoke."*

The next few months were fraught with pain and high fever, as the wound refused to heal. He was shipped back to Australia in January 1919, but died during the voyage and was buried at sea near Colombo.

I have the piece of explosive shell which he refers to in the letter.

No.2 Australian Hospital Ship.

H.M.A.H.S."KANOWNA"

Feb. 4th 1919.

From O.C.Troops H.M.A.H.S."KANOWNA"
To Mr. John Scott
      Lerwick
            Shetland Islands
                  Scotland.

Dear Sir,

It is my sad duty to tell you of the death of your Son. Bertram Scott. He was carried on board the "Kanowna" at Southampton 5th January in a very poor condition suffering from shell wounds, right leg (fractured tibia).

He was operated on and had leg amputated just below the knee, on 28th January. The operation was very successful, but the lad seemed to lose heart, and in spite of all that could be done for him, he sank and died at 7.p.m on 1st February.

He was buried in the Arabian Sea, the funeral services being sympathetically performed by Rev. Chaplain Bath, in the presence of a large number of the poor boy's comrades.

He was devotedly attended to by Capt. McKay (A.A.M.C) and nursed by Sister Ryan and Staff Nurse Laycook.

Please accept our expression of deep sympathy with you in the loss which you have sustained.

Yours very sincerely,

H.Mackenzie .... Lt.Col.
O.C.Troops H.M.A.H.S."KANOWNA"

Bertie's Dream

It is part of our family's lore that Bertie had foreseen his own death in a vivid dream shortly before he emigrated to Australia. The extract below was written to my grandfather in 1932 by his father (Captain John Scott), who had gone out after the war to join his sons Donnie, Willie, Jamie, Bobby and Sammy. The "Shetland Times" was posted out to him each week.

Did you notice in the "Times" 12th of Oct
I think about a man having a
Dream about the "Ben dorn" Disester
a week befor it Hapned on the
Vee-Skerries. It put Something in
my mind that I will tell you
Jamie told me after we came here
one night when him & Bertie Slept
in that little room above the front
Door. That Bertie awoke him one
night crying bitterly. He Said he
Dreamed He was onboard a large
Steamer. He was not one of the crew
& He was not a passenger.

He did not seame to know what
He was But he thought he died
& was buried at sea.
now here is a dream that
actuly took place.
Kindest love to all
from your Loving father

John Scott MBE

A Matter of Time

Time is no more
Than a gossamer curtain,
A mere breath of air
Makes it shift and sway.

It lifts and we see things
That have not yet happened,
We hear ourselves speak words
We have yet to say.

We feel future pain,
Future fear or elation.
Tomorrow's emotions
Are with us today.

Time's curtain moves,
We slip back into history,
Experience events
That took place yesterday

For Time is not fixed.
We move backwards and forwards.
Our past and our future
Are part of today.

Stones

Is it the scale of the slaughter that hurts us,
So many graveyards, so many white stones?
Or is it the age of the young boys who lie here
Cried out for their mothers, but faced death alone.

Or the stark uniformity of the inscriptions –
Name, rank and number and date ... if they're known?
Or the sadness surrounding those two words "a soldier"
On tombs where they've laid unidentified bones?

Or the thousands of names of the thousands of "missing"
Who left thousands of loved ones unable to mourn ...
For "missing", not "dead", gave room for wild fancies –
Each click of the latch could mean he has come home ...

I stand here and take on the guilt of survivors
Who saw comrades die, but got through and lived on;
My heart lifts and quickens with false hopes of sweethearts
Whose lives have no meaning without their loved ones.

My back bears the burden of sorrowing mothers,
I grieve with the fathers who outlived their sons
For each soldier's story's a stone in a millpond.
Its ripples spread outward long after he's gone.

This is only a section of Tyne Cot Cemetery, which is the largest British Military Cemetery in the world. It is built on the forward slope of the Passchendaele ridge. This area was named "Tyne Cot" by the Northumberland Fusiliers, who thought the square shapes of the German "pillboxes" looked like Tyneside cottages.

He died at Arras,
The grandfather young enough
To be my grandson.

Commonwealth War Graves

The landscape of northern France (and of Belgium) is dotted with war cemeteries. A visit to any of these burial places is deeply moving and cannot be described in words. Perhaps the most disturbing aspect of it is the tender age at which so many soldiers died.

Unknown

Commonwealth graves of unknown soldiers were inscribed A SOLDIER OF THE GREAT WAR; and, at the foot of the stone, KNOWN UNTO GOD.

Inconnu

The crosses which mark the grave of French unknown soldiers simply say INCONNU.

Burial at Sea

John (Donnie) Scott – eldest brother – was very close to my grandfather, and they exchanged long thoughtful letters from the time he went to sea, particularly after he settled in Australia.

This is a transcription of part of one of his letters, which describes his world view, and sets the scene for a poem he wrote:

"Now while you have been tramping up and down the Garrison Close and I roaming the face of the Globe, I have come to the conclusion that life is not what I thought it would be but it is in a great measure what you make it yourself, and the only way to enjoy a medium share of happiness is to try and be content with your lot and struggle on doing your best wherever you are. You say you envy me in some things viz. having seen the world. I assure you this is nothing to envy … It is not when the wind is howling and there's danger to life and limb that I envy you. I rather enjoy the excitement, but it is on a night like the present when I get the blues. I can picture you sitting at your fireside with a book, or amusing the children, surrounded by all you hold dear … while I sit here all alone in a cabin 12ft by 6ft, everyone ashore with their friends while all my dear ones are hundreds of miles away and unget-atable … I have certainly seen more of the world than you, but it is a question whether I know more of the world than you. Books are splendid teachers. I often wish I had your headgear to take in what I read like you do, so old man there's not much to envy me over and I would change places with you any day. I often think if I could write a history of my chequered career, it would be worth reading … but the more you go through and the more you see and have to endure the less you feel like talking or writing about it … as much as to say, what's the use of talking about it, folks wouldn't understand. I honestly believe that when the history of the last 4 ½ years is written, it won't be by men who have gone through the mill but by the lookers on … I think you must have infected me with the philosophic germ …"

He encloses a copy of the poem, and describes the event which inspired it.

"One of our boys (troops) died. I was officiating at his burial and when getting back to my duty on the bridge, thinking over the circumstances, I took my pencil and wrote the enclosed … I'm not extolling it as poetry, but it expresses the feelings of us all at the time."

Gone West (Donnie's Poem)

Our craft lay quiet on the vast gray deep,
The flag, at stern, hung drooping at the dip,
All nature seemed attuned with us to keep
The mournful silence, brooding oíer the ship.

For there beneath the flag he'd fought for, lay,
So still and silent, in his long last rest,
Our comrade, yet not he, but only clay
Of him, who's soul had taken flight out west.

The chaplain read with sad and solemn air,
The words o'er him who in Death's arms did sleep
And then with rifle shot and bugle's blare,
The body was committed to the deep.

No costly casket covered his brave breast,
Just rolled in canvas, sewn by sailor men,
And thus upon the ocean's bed he'll rest,
Until the sea gives up its dead again.

An Anzac lad, a patriot to the core,
One of the best, a soldier clean and true,
He'd done his bit, but volunteered once more,
To go and help his comrades oíer the blue.

But he's gone west, his fighting days are done,
We mourn our loss, our loss that is his gain,
And there with comrades who have fought and won,
He'll wait for us, and welcome us again.

The Menin Gate

The Menin Gate is a vast arch which spans the Menin Road as it enters the town of Ypres. On its walls are the names of 54,896 soldiers who fell in the Ypres Salient before 15/8/17, and who have no known grave.

The Last Post was played here at the opening ceremony on 24/7/27. It was sounded again on 11/11/29, and at 8 p.m. every night since (except during the German occupation in the Second World War). It is played by buglers from the local Fire Brigade. The ceremony is poignant, reverent and thought-provoking – and everyone who witnesses it is affected by it.

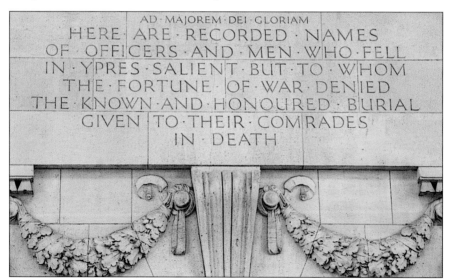

AD · MAJOREM · DEI · GLORIAM
HERE ARE · RECORDED · NAMES OF · OFFICERS · AND · MEN · WHO · FELL IN · YPRES · SALIENT · BUT · TO · WHOM THE · FORTUNE · OF · WAR · DENIED THE · KNOWN · AND · HONOURED · BURIAL GIVEN TO · THEIR · COMRADES IN · DEATH

Tyne Cot and Thiepval

On the wall behind Tyne Cot cemetery are the names of 34,888 soldiers who fell in the Ypres Salient after 15/8/17, and have no known grave – there was no room left on the Menin Gate.

The memorial at Thiepval was designed by Sir Edward Lutyens. On the faces of its sixteen massive piers are the names of 73,412 British and South African soldiers who fell at the Somme between 1/7/15 and 20/3/18, and who have no known grave.

The Caribou

Outlined against the sky she stands
The Caribou of Newfoundland.
She scents the foreign air, surveys
The unfamiliar fields and bays
Her everlasting, pain-wracked song –
A requiem for her lost young.

Memorial Parks

Beaumont Hamel

The great bronze sculpture of a caribou (the emblem of the Newfoundland Regiment) stands on a rocky mound in the Newfoundland Memorial park near Beaumont Hamel. At the bottom of the mound are three bronze plaques which bear the names of the missing – 591 officers and men of the Royal Newfoundland Regiment, 114 of the Newfoundland Royal Naval Reserve and 115 of the Newfoundland Mercantile Marine.

The park contains a system of preserved trenches, which show the typical zig-zag construction. Although these are grassed over there is something chilling about them when one looks over the parapet across No Man's Land toward enemy lines. Here and there are the iron pickets which supported the barbed wire. The ground is pitted and cratered, evidence of violent fighting. The only cover was the shell-holes. Halfway between the British front line and Y-Ravine (where the Germans had positioned their machine guns) is a solitary tree, or rather its petrified remains. It is known as the Danger Tree, for it was here that the Newfoundlanders suffered their greatest loss. It is a poignant symbol which imprints itself on the mind.

Vimy Ridge (see overleaf)

This monument is impressive and affecting. It commemorates not only the 3,598 Canadians who died in the Battle of Vimy Ridge, but all Canadians who fought in the Great War. On the walls are the names of the 11,258 missing.

The design was chosen from 160 submitted, and was the creation of a Toronto sculptor, Walter S. Allward. It consists of two massive pylons (representing Canada and France), with several heroic figures placed round it to symbolise Peace, Justice, Truth, Knowledge and the Spirit of Canada.

It is confusing in that you approach the monument from the rear, though it doesn't seem so – and the Spirit of Canada (which would appear to be at the back) is really at the front. I prefer to think of her as having withdrawn to be by herself, with her own private grief … behind the others – not the main focus!

The monument stands in the Canadian Memorial park, which also has a system of preserved trenches – the sandbags reconstructed in concrete. On the Allied slope of the ridge is a network of tunnels – 22 miles in all, on four different levels. On the lowest was a railway for transporting ammunition. One can enter the Grange tunnel and walk through the 800 yards on the top level, marvelling at the level of sophistication – electric lighting, water pumps, ventilation shafts and pumps, and little "rooms" at the sides which served as offices, standing rooms, stores etc.. Its purpose was to bring troops in safety close up to the front line.

The Spirit of Canada

Twin flags
blatter in the wind.
They snap and crack.
Their kaleidoscope
of broken patterns
gives and takes back
ever-changing elements
of Maple Leaf
and Fleur-de-Lis.

Ropes hum and vibrate.
Their metal gear clicks
against slender poles
that are tall as the masts
of ocean-going clipper ships.
Signs ask for reverence.
We talk in whispers,
as the long straight paths
draw us to the monument.

Solid ... unshakable ...
It dwarfs and humbles us
with its stark statement
against the blue sky.

I reach out and touch
the tight texture of letters,
trace with my fingers
the bleak truth of names
incised with precise
and painstaking devotion,
into the ice-coldness
of Croatian stone.

Behind, robed for ever
in soft folds of sorrow,
the Spirit of Canada
bears her grief alone,
for pride merely cloaks
the pain of a nation
whose children died
thousands of miles
from their home.

Don't stray from the paths.
These innocent fields still hold
Grim relics of war

Iron Harvest

During the war 14 billion rounds of ammunition were fired – 1.4 billion did not go off. 200 - 250 are found each year, usually by farmers as they plough their fields. 10% of these shells contain toxic gas. The relics are placed at the edge of their fields for the bomb squad to collect and dispose of. They deal with 20 shells a day. In 1986 four bomb disposal men were blown up, and every year members of the public are injured or killed. Tourists are warned not to touch the "Iron Harvest", but many are tempted to take home "souvenirs".

Soldiers in the front also sent home souvenirs. For example there are brass shell cases which serve as vases, pencil holders or ornaments in many homes! Smaller shells were often made into cigarette lighters. Grenades were defused and sent home, but in many cases they had not been emptied of their powder which, with the passage of time, became unstable. One such grenade spent many years in my grandmother's china cabinet before being wrapped in newspaper and stored in a cupboard. We found it there in 1985, 70 years after it had beem sent home (see page 93).

Military Honours

From time to time bodies of soldiers are found, which is not really surprising when one considers the vast numbers who disappeared without trace – who drowned in shell-holes, were covered by the debris of explosions, or sank beneath the mud round Ypres.

In April 1998, three First War soldiers were buried at a village near Arras. They died on 11 April, 1917 – the third day of the Battle of Arras (a week after Frankie's death). Their bodies were discovered in a mass grave by archaeologists working at Monchy-le-Preux. Two were identified by their dog-tags. The third remains unknown. They served with the 13th Battalion Royal Fusiliers.

They were given a full military burial, attended by about 200 people. Among those present was First War veteran, Harry Wells (98) who survived the Battle of Arras. He spent two years in hospital, suffering from the effects of mustard gas. He was told in 1920 that if he gave up wine, women and song he might live for another 10 years!

In May this year an Australian soldier was buried , again with full military honours.

Strange Harvest

Beside ploughed fields – the Iron Harvest.
Rusty casings, leaking gas,
Clips of bullets, broken fuses.
Keep away. "Ne touchez pas."

Tractor finds a human body,
Grinning skull and scattered bones.
Search until you find his dog-tag.
He must not remain "unknown".

Carve his name upon the headstone.
Erase it from the Tyne Cot wall.
Bury him with pride and honour,
Holy words and trumpet-call.

Let his aged sons and daughters,
Slowed by their advancing years,
Make their way with wreaths of poppies.
Let them weep for wasted years.

Souvenirs

The clip of bullets and the grenade
were neatly wrapped in a crumpled page
of the "Times" – a Special War Edition –
torn and faded, yellowed with age.
The bomb lay, egg-shaped, in my hand.
Unnerved, I feared that I might see
some raptor-chick with hate-filled eye
break out and glare at me ...

Police and then the bomb-squad came,
business-like, efficient, bluff.
"Powder that's as old as this
is sure to be unstable stuff,"
The explosion was professional,
controlled and carefully planned,
fragments neatly held within
a strong container filled with sand ...

and I thought I heard the blast of a shell,
remembered a "Digger" whose own fragments fell
like rain on a valley near Jericho
yesterday – several lifetimes ago ...
a boy who longed to see Shetland again,
but passed too soon "out of the sight of men",
age-old in experience, but tender in years,
the boy who collected these grim "souvenirs".

Nostalgia

The extract below refers to Arab camel drivers, and comes from Tommy's last letter which was written on 12/7/18 (two days before he was killed). His mood is uncharacteristic, full of nostalgia. He complains that he hasn't heard from home for weeks and weeks, asks about "wir boat" and uses the dialect. Strangely, my grandfather's last letter to him (which was returned to him unread) told about the boat.

HE whom this scroll commemorates was numbered among those who, at the call of King and Country, left all that was dear to them, endured hardness, faced danger, and finally passed out of the sight of men by the path of duty and self-sacrifice, giving up their own lives that others might live in freedom.

Let those who come after see to it that his name be not forgotten.

Cpl. Thomas Moffat Scott.
1 L.H.R. A.I.F.

THE END OF THE WAR
How the News Reached Lerwick.

When it became known that the German delegates had got till Monday afternoon to sign the Armistice terms, feeling ran high. It had been stated that the agreement would be decided on Sunday, and there was a tense feeling of anxiety manifested all through the community as to what the result would be. All through the afternoon and evening of Sunday anxious questions were put as to the latest news from the front. But no intimation was made, and it was not until Monday morning that the gratifying information reached Lerwick that Germany had accepted the terms laid down to her, that she had signed the Armistice, and that hostilities were to cease at 11 o'clock that day.

The first local intimation reached Rear-Admiral Greatorex, C.B., M.V.O., by wireless, and he immediately sent his information to the 'Shetland Times' Office - for which on behalf of the community we tender him our sincere thanks - and thereafter, we displayed, shortly after 9 a.m., a placard in our office window in Commercial Street, announcing the good news. It at once attracted a crowd. People from all parts came and read the good news, and went away filled with joy that at length the end had come, and victory had crowned the efforts of Britain and her Allies.

When the intimation came through the Central News Agency, we at once had a small hand-bill printed in the following terms :-

THE PRIME MINISTER MAKES THE FOLLOWING ANNOUNCEMENT :-
THE ARMISTICE WAS SIGNED AT 6 O'CLOCK THIS MORNING,
AND HOSTILITIES CEASE ON ALL FRONTS AT 11 A.M. TO-DAY.

An appeal for distributors met with a hearty response from Mr Durham, headmaster of the Central School and he placed a willing and eager corps of schoolboys at our disposal. Thousands of copies were printed and handed free to every house in Lerwick and to all the inhabitants and visitors.

The news was received with deep, unspeakable pleasure by all, but there were no indications of hilarity. The strain had been too great, the tension too strong to permit of levity. There was no pretence at what is commonly described as 'popular' rejoicings. It was with subdued feelings, a sensation that ran too deep for words, that people met each other, and with genuine hand-clasps congratulated each other that the maiming and killing of the war were at an end.

The Shetland Times, Saturday, 16 November, 1918.

Armistice

In this extract Donnie gives his view of the Armistice from his ship tied up in Tilbury Docks:

"Peace will soon be signed and we will be able to go on our way without a queer feeling creeping up your spine every time a neesick bools under your bows. They are having a great time in London. Up-Helly-Aa isn't in it. I was up town on Saturday night and the row was awful, traffic was suspended to allow the people to make merry. They made so merry that they nearly destroyed Nelson's monument by fire, and then burned down some of the captured guns so their jollifications have been curtailed somewhat, but what does anything matter. The war is over. What it is going to be after the war remains to be seen, but it is sufficient for the present to know that the struggle is over. Amen."

neesick = porpoise
bools = jumps through the surface of the water
Up-Helly-Aa = fire festival held in Lerwick every January

AUSTRALIAN AUXILIARY HOSPITAL No. 1,
HAREFIELD PARK,
HAREFIELD,
MIDDLESEX.

18-11-18

Dear Lottie

It is some time since I wrote you last but I get very tired writing and absolutely no news to write about. My leg is improving steadily every day it shows a little improvement and I am hoping if all goes well I aught to be home for Christmas but with a wound like mine you never can tell what it will do next. I had a big surprise on Saturday when Donnie walked in to see me He is looking A1 and much stouter than he was when I saw him last that is over two years ago Well I don't know what more I can tell you I expect Donnie and all the boys write you so you know more about them than I do. Everybody about here seen to have gone mad about this armistice I see they have been having some royal times in London it is a good job it is over if I could only get out of this blessed hospital I would be as happy as anybody Well I think that is all my news meantime Heaps love to you all

Yours Affec Bros
Bertie.

PS
Thank you for the paper received alright the other day. Enclosed is a notice I got the other day at present I am marked up for 100% pension

B

Rebuilding Lives

Life after the war would never be the same again. On the personal level, many had lost loved ones and had to cope with all that bereavement brings. My grandfather lost three younger brothers.

Others had to provide short and long term care for their wounded relatives, which they willingly did. The following transcript from a letter from John shows his intention to care for Bertie:

"What you mentioned I'm afraid is only too true. Of course there's nothing to be alarmed about. I don't know if the boy knows himself but the operation he went through in Melbourne was from the effects of Tuberculosis, and by what I can find out from Bertie himself, I know it's the disease in his system that's hampering the healing of his leg so the sooner he can get fit to travel and can get out to Australia the better I'll like it ... for the climate there will soon set him up. It doesn't matter whether he will be fit for work or not. It's up to me to see him through, and the sooner he get's out to Jeannie's care the more I'll be pleased. He's done his best and he knows he has a home in Melbourne to come to ..."

As we have seen, Bertie died on the way to Australia. Willie did return, but with a damaged heart as a result of being buried alive at Passchendaele. He made his home with John and his wife, Jeannie, and took up carpentry as his trade. He had served his apprenticeship with Shearer's (cabinet-makers) in Lerwick. He no longer had the stamina for fruit-farming, which he'd done before the war.

Sammy jilted the girl he had intended to marry, and emigrated to Australia after the war. He was restless, and found it difficult to stay in one place (or one job) for long. He was out of touch with the family sometimes for several years at a time. He suffered all the rest of his life from the effects of mustard gas.

Returning soldiers were unable to speak of their experiences with civilian friends and family, for those who had not been there could not envisage the magnitude of the horror. This created a chasm between husbands and wives, and between friends.

For many, peacetime brought emotional, physical and financial problems, but there are countless stories of hardship borne with uncomplaining fortitude, selfless devotion and enduring love.

What then?

After the flag waving,
After the hip-hoorays,
After the sounds of singing
And church-bells have died away
For some joyful reunion
But happy tears betray
The sorrowing for whom there is
No celebration day ...

For what good is the Armistice
To those whose loved ones lie
And rot in putrid shell-holes
Beneath a foreign sky?
Or the girl who seeks her hero,
Marching home with head held high
But finds a shuffling stranger
With trembling lip and vacant eye?

What freedom for the wounded,
The limbless and the blind?
For the broken man, the shell-shocked,
Imprisoned by his tortured mind?
What peace for those who love them?
What comfort can they find
When all their hopes lie withered
With the dreams they've left behind?

After the flag-waving,
After the hip-hoorays,
After the sounds of singing
And church-bells have died away ...
What then? So many secrets,
So much they could not say,
So much special courage
As they face each brave new day.

Broken Faces

For me "Les Gueules Cassées" (Men with broken faces) symbolise not only the worst that war and hatred can do, but also the magnificent force of human love. To accept without pity – and love – a man whose face is so disfigured that he is unrecognisable and frightening to look at, is a triumph of the human spirit.

Many underwent repeated surgery, and reconstructive techniques made rapid advances. The problems, however, were not only physical, but also psychological. To spare them the shock, sighted victims were often denied a mirror whilst in hospital. This meant that they (along with blind victims) had no idea what they looked like, nor were they prepared for the effect their appearance would have on others. The truth, when they learned it, was often traumatic.

Those whose faces could not be rebuilt were sometimes given a mask to wear to hide their disfigurement, and enable them to take their place in society again. Many, however, could not cope and commited suicide.

The following anecdote describes the situation when a M. Lazé, who was severely disfigured (and also blind), went home for the first time. He was accompanied by his nurse, Henriette Rémi – who gave this account in "Hommes sans Visages", which is quoted in "1914-1918 The Great War and the Shaping of the 20th Century" by Jay Winter and Blaine Baggett.

His wife welcomed him at the door and called their son, Gérard. The boy uttered a piercing cry: the boy shook. His father was shaken too … Gérard turned and ran … crying in a loud voice; "That's not Papa." Lazé was desolate.

Henriette went to comfort the boy. He was shaking … He hid in his mother's skirts. Lazé was rooted to the spot. He took his head in his hands and said: "Imbécile. Imbécile! But how could I have known how horrible I am. Someone should have told me!"

Back at the hospital he told Henriette, "Having once been a man, I am now an object of terror to my own son, a daily burden to my wife, a shameful thing to all humanity."

A second visit resulted in the same cries, "That's not Papa." Lazé recoiled. "It's finished. It's too late. I terrify him." That night, back in hospital, he committed suicide.

La Gueule Cassée

When he came home
she held her breath
while the world turned
in a dizzy spinning.

When it stood still
she held out her arms
to the man whose face
was beyond reconstruction.

The child hid his face
in her skirts screaming
"Take him away, he isn't my Dad!"
and pummelled her thighs
with tight fists of terror.

The man with no mouth
had questions in his eyes.
She gave him a mirror.
"No-one told me," he said,
with eloquent fingers.

They made him a mask
to cover the remnants
of muscle and bone ...

"I knew that the other man
couldn't be you," said the child
to the face that he wore
for the world.

In the dark she explored
the grotesque geography
of absent features
and they learned to make love
without words or kissing.

Bereft

When he died
She became sorrow,
No longer a woman
But an aching pain.
Her body dissolved in it,
And her brain ...

Her spirit sought his
In mountain and stone,
In river and stream,
And in the long straight line
Of sea meets sky.

She couldn't find him,
Only the chill wind
Of never-ending loneliness
And the dark abyss
Of loveless years.

She folded her wings
And plummeted down
To drown in the deep well
Of forgetfulness.

Oblivion welcomed her,
Drained all the pain from her
Till she was nothing.
In that she found peace.

The Ballad of Mary Martin

One day as I was walking
Along a country lane
I saw a rainbow on the ground
And stopped to look again.
No rainbow, but a garden
With flowers of every hue!
I asked a woman passing by
If she could tell me who

Had made this piece of Paradise
For I would like to meet
The one who had the skill to weave
This living carpet at my feet.
She looked at me with troubled eye,
And then began her tale to tell
About the girl who'd fashioned Heaven
From out of her own private Hell.

"Her name is Mary Martin ..."
My pulse began to race
For I had heard that name before ...
Another time – another place.
And all the while a sweet voice
Floated on the scented air,
Wrought a spell around my heart,
Kept me willing captive there.

The Woman's Tale

Once Mary had a sweetheart
Who did not want to fight.
He did not hold with warfare.
She convinced him it was right.
She said that every man must do
His bit for country and for king –
That if he shirked his duty
She must give him back his ring ...

And I, spurred on by foolish pride,
Gave him the coward's feather.
I bade him go – so she and I,
We bear the guilt together ...
The woman paused to dry her eyes,
Then said, "I'll end what I've begun,
But oh it is so painful, sir –
You see he was my only son."

From out her apron pocket
She took a tear-stained note,
And haltingly she read to me
The useless, empty words I wrote ...
"It's my duty to inform you ..."
And "It is with deep regret ..."
Familiar, standard phrases –
How could I forget?

I murmured, "Private Johnson,
Number one-oh-seven-three-oh,
Died of wounds near Passchendaele ..."
She stared at me. "How did you know?"
And all the while a sweet voice
Floated on the scented air,
Wrought a spell around my heart,
Kept me willing captive there.

The Soldier's Tale

I went to be a soldier.
I learned I must obey
All orders to the letter,
Was taught to kill in different ways.
So "Yes sir, no sir. Three bags full" –
I left many maimed or dead
Until a voice screamed "Murderer!"
Inside my battle-weary head.

Christ said, "All men are brothers."
I could not bear the weight
Of shame that pressed upon me,
For I had not learned to hate.
I knew every Bosche I'd shot
Was some poor grieving mother's son.
And so I wiped my bayonet
And, weeping, threw away my gun.

I wandered into No-man's-land.
There I knelt and tried to pray
"Deliver us from evil, Lord."
And "Father, take my sins away ..."
And all the while her sweet voice
Floated on the smoke-filled air,
Brought strength to my failing heart
As they took me captive there.

The Officer's Tale

The trial was a mockery ...
Men must be made to fear
The law more than the gas-cloud.
On this the General's mind was clear.
"As a soldier you've no value,
You're a coward through and through.
No place in this man's army
For squeamish lads like you.

You'll serve as an example.
Have you anything to say?"
The boy just said, "Thou shalt not kill."
The General snapped, "Take him away."
In vain I asked for mercy.
I vouched for him, "As his C.O.
I've seen him show great courage ..." but
They did not want to know.

I spent his last night with him,
And oh the hours were long,
But when he made his last request
His voice was firm and strong ...
"Please go to Mary Martin sir.
Tell her I'd no fear of death.
Say her name was on my lips
As I breathed my final breath."

They led him out in dawn's grey light.
He walked tall, his head held high.
He said, "I'll have no blindfold sir."
I could not look him in the eye ...
They pinned a target to his chest,
Tied him roughly to the post.
The priest droned, "Spiritu sanctu ...
Father, Son and Holy Ghost."

His comrades took their aim and fired.
The birds in nearby woods took flight.
They circled round – I watched until
They disappeared from human sight.
And all the while a sweet voice
Floated on the morning air,
Bringing comfort to my heart
As I stood a-weeping there.

The Meeting

"You are that man," the woman said.
"You share our guilt. That is your fate ...
I'll take you now to Mary sir."
She paused, her hand upon the gate,
"You'll find she's like a child sir.
She's not as other women are –
Her mind has been sore wounded.
It bears a raw, unhealing scar, ..."

105

"Good morning, Mary Martin.
"How does your garden grow?"
"Thank you, kind sir, for asking
But I've many seeds to sow –
There's Poppies for the soldiers
Who died in Picardy,
And Cornflowers for the sailor-boys
Who lie beneath the sea.

There's Lily-of-the-Valley,
Some call it 'Mother's Tears',
It's scent will lead them up to Heaven
And take away their fears.
I must plant healing Yarrow
And Violets for heart's-ease
For every day there's something
That someone must tell the bees.

The Daisies – they're for innocence –
For simple folk like me,
Folk who cannot understand
Why such sorrow has to be ..."
I said, "I've come to tell you
That your sweetheart loved you so,
And at the end he whispered ..."
"Hush, sir," she said. "I know

For every day at dawning
The birds rise from the trees
And circle, bringing tender words
From my true love to me ...
Now, if you will excuse me sir,
I'll bid 'Good-day' to you –
There's little time for talking
When there's so much work to do.

There's Marigolds for cheerfulness,
Pansies for secret thoughts,
Roses ... and an ocean
Of blue Forget-me-nots."
And all the while her sweet voice
Floated on the scented air.
It wove a spell around my heart.
I left it willing captive there.

Rebuilding

Churchill wanted Ypres to be left in ruins as evidence of the destructive power of war. The townspeople had other ideas. The town was rebuilt exactly as it was before. The Cloth Hall was restored according to the original plans. The cost was borne by Germany – one of the conditions of the Treaty of Versailles.

Ypres then.

Ypres now.

Ypres

Ypres was the shining eye
Beneath the threatening brow of hills
That curved from Kemmel eastwards,
Then north to Passchendaele.

Three times they tried to gouge it out.
Three times they left it scarred and maimed,
Surrounded by a sea of mud –
But still they could not douse the flame

That burned beneath the ravaged Church,
The ruins of the great Cloth Hall,
The rubble that was Butterstreet,
The Market Place, the city walls

For this spark flared so fiercely
It consumed dark history
And proved that where there is the will
Then anything can be ...

Now crowds collect each evening
Beneath the Menin Gate
To listen to the fanfare,
And in silence contemplate ...

Remembering the thousands
Of brave unfamous men,
And the spirit of this city
That resolved to rise again.

Double Exposure

We sat in the square at Cambrai
Tables, umbrellas, the warmth of the sun.
Vin rouge, Andouillettes,
Et des frites, s'il vous plaît.

"Smile!" "Salut!" I raised my glass,
And wondered if his camera
Would catch the buildings as they are –
These brave, defiant replicas ...

Or would I be a shadow cast
On smoking rubble, rumbling tanks?
Just one more ghost to join the ranks
Of those who haunt this cobbled "place".

Replanting

Forests and farmlands had to be reclaimed and replanted. This was a difficult and dangerous task because of the number of unexploded bombs and ammunition which lay above and below the ground. Farmers added metal plates beneath their tractor-seats to give some protection. Even today injuries occur during the ploughing season.

Disease was also a hazard due to the amount of putrescence in the soil; and, until drainage was restored, the muddy quagmires presented the same problems to the farmworkers as had been experienced by the soldiers.

Old Photograph (1916)

Leafing through history,
I saw silhouettes
Of wounded trees.
Charred and naked they rose
Like blackened cacti
From a slough of mud,
Where tin helmets
Grew in clusters –
Obscene fungi
Feeding on the dead.

Colour Reversal

War makes the landscape
Wear widow's weeds.
Her dress is mud-coloured.
A veil of smoke covers her face
Now pitted, and grey
As gas-vapour.

A gunshot. Blood spurts through
The rough weft of fabric,
Leaves garish splashes
On sackcloth and ashes
And life seeps away
Like a spillage of wine.

trees

don't let memories

render them impotent

war upon war

could not break their spirit

or prevent their cycle of regeneration

but they have not forgotten

for each year in autumn they show us their grief

transformed into a triumph of red and gold

this is their answer

to blood

and fire

John McCrae

John McCrae, a Canadian surgeon, served as a medical officer in the Ypres salient. He wrote one of the best-known poems of the Great War – "In Flanders' Fields". It was largely due to this poem that the poppy was adopted as the symbol of remembrance.

Whilst on a Battlefields Tour, I was asked to read the poem to our group on the very spot where it was written, i.e. beside the dressing station at Essex Farm (see photograph below). I found it a deeply moving experience.

In Flanders Fields

In Flanders fields the poppies blow
Between the crosses row on row
That mark our place; and in the sky
The larks, still bravely singing, fly
Scarce heard amid the guns below.

We are the Dead. Short days ago
We lived, felt dawn, saw sunset glow,
Loved and were loved, and now we lie
In Flanders fields.

Take up our quarrel with the foe:
To you from failing hands we throw
The torch; be yours to hold it high.
If ye break faith with us who die
We shall not sleep, though poppies grow
In Flanders fields.

by John McCrae

For John McCrae

I feel your presence near me
As I read your words aloud
While larks, "still bravely singing, fly"
Above the listening crowd.

We blink back tears, remember
The plea you made long years ago –
You who lived, "loved, and were loved",
"Felt dawn and saw (the) sunset glow".

No crosses now, but headstones
Mark the places, row on row,
Of you who sleep in Flanders' Fields,
In Flanders' Fields where poppies blow.

Snapshot of Nineties Man

We are the hard men.
We scorn the soft focus
Of tenderness.
It blurs the sharp edge
Of objectivity,
Diffuses our drive
Toward personal goals.

We cannot be duped
By stirring words.
We sneer at innocence
And grand abstractions
Like "love" and "duty".
"Give us the proof," we say.
"Surely everyone asks
'What's in it for us?'
And weighs up the odds?"

We are the hard men,
We take without giving.
We are the heartless.
Unloved and unloving.
We are the soul-less,
Our goals were worth nothing.
Think on us ... pity us ...
Pray for us.

Remembrance

Every town and community throughout the country raised a memorial to commemorate their local "boys" who fell in the war. This serves as a focus for acts of remembrance which take place on Remembrance Sunday each year.

Some people consider these ceremonies glorify war, and should no longer take place. I think it is right to honour those who gave their lives, and also those who survived and suffered for the rest of their lives in ways we can only imagine.

Unveiling The Shetland War Memorial at Lerwick, 6th January, 1924. Photo. by R. H. Ramsay.

THEIR NAME LIVETH FOR EVERMORE

Bones

Between the lines
In No-man's-land
Corpses moulder
And blacken in the sun ...
Cover them gently
And leave them to rest.

Between the lines
Of written words
Are buried truths.
Dig up these bones
And learn from them.
Do not let them rest.

Research

At first inside my head I see
Your dim, reflected history –
Not you, but a dark shadow of
The man you were, the man who loved
These gleaming lochs; these glistening hills;
This shining ocean, winter-still;
This arching, star-strewn northern sky;
Its mirrored moon as much as I ...

You must not walk from off the page,
Insubstantial, blurred with age.

I'll set my mind's technology
To work on faded imagery.
I'll sharpen focus, make it clear;
Sweep away the mist of years;
Search behind your censored words,
Flesh out their bones. I'll lower your guard
So that you'll show me when clouds part
The pulse of truth within your heart.

Photographic Evidence

He marches with soldiers, but carries no gun.
His job is to show how each victory is won.
His weapon's a Kodak. He's not trained to kill,
But he brings to the battle his own special skill.

His duty's to capture events as they are,
Record the realities of the Great War.
His prisoners are pictures of brave fighting men.
He fires all his shots through a camera lens.

The penalty's death should he dare to show
Things that the war-lords don't want us to know.
His orders are clear. "We don't want you to lie,
But there's no need to show how our young soldiers die.

Avoid scenes of carnage, don't show disillusion
Or boys who've lost heart, don't show the confusion,
Don't show the dismembered, don't show the blood
Or the waste of young lives for a metre of mud.

You must be selective. You mustn't offend
The great British public on whom we depend
For replacement recruits who are willing to do
Whatever we Generals order them to."

* * * * * * * * * * *

He marched with the soldiers, though he had no gun.
He truthfully told how each battle was won.
He knew the risks, but he conquered his fears
And eighty years on he still triggers our tears.

But his silent witness is only the start.
History isn't the sum of its parts.
A leaf's not a tree, nor a petal a flower.
One wave's not the sea, nor a minute an hour.

One star's a mere speck in a whole constellation.
One instant can't give us enough information.
One click of the shutter can't possibly tell
What led to, or followed, that moment of Hell

For he can't let us hear their words or their screams.
We only can guess at their nightmares, their dreams.
We don't have to live in a waterlogged trench
With flesh-fattened rats. We can't feel the stench.

We can't share their terror, their stark disbelief,
Their burden of guilt when they couldn't feel grief
As their pals fell around them. Their senses were numb
For shock stole their reason and silenced their tongues.

But he makes us confront it. He makes us ask why
Young men in their millions were sent out to die.
He shows through his anger, his sorrow, his shame
That the War-to-end-wars was "Great" only in name.

Stained Glass Windows

The Basilica of Notre Dame d'Espérance is in Charleville-Mézières which is on the French-Belgian border in the Ardennes. The building was damaged by fire in the French Revolution, by cannons in 1815 and 1870, and by shells and bombs in both world wars.

The entire building has been restored in its original Gothic style with magnificent pillars and arches. The 1000 square metres of stained glass are entirely new. They are modern and abstract in design, yet they marry perfectly with their surroundings. It took the artist, René Dürrbach, from 1954 to 1979 to complete the sixty-six windows. He used colour, shape and number to symbolise all aspects of the Catholic creed. These are arranged around the dualism of hope and despair, as represented by La Vierge d'Espérance and La Vierge Noire.

The immediate effect is utterly stunning, and empties the mind of everything else. Then one is able to study each window in turn, and seek out its meaning. It is a work which is unique in Europe.

This window is the first in the sequence, and shows the balanced pattern of creation. The four elements are represented in colour – earth is yellow, fire is red, air is white and water is blue.

In all the windows, circles and curves symbolise the spiritual dimension and the God-created, while squares and straight lines stand for everything created by man.

Notre Dame d'Espérance

Silence steadies me.
Its strong arms enfold me
While the explosion of light and colour
Rocks the foundations of my non-belief
And the old is made new
In shape and number.

The serpent weaves its tortuous path
Through the balanced pattern of creation ...
From order comes chaos, darkness from light
And we lose ourselves in the labyrinth
Of human weakness.

The smooth ovoid of new beginnings
Brings spiralling hope, and widening
Circles of everlasting love.
Earth and heaven are joined
By the bold perpendicular
Of a purple Christ.

A soft sea of blue
Bathes the Cross at Golgotha
As the Mother brings comfort
To her suffering Son. Then the fours
Of elements, compass-points, seasons
Rejoice in the wonder
Of Three-become-One.

The Spirit brings peace
To twelve grieving Apostles
Who glow with the glory of Pentecost's fire
But joy walks with sadness, hope with despair
As La Vierge d'Espérance bows to La Vierge Noire
For the Father all-seeing, all-knowing, all-loving
Has not the power – or the will –
To end war.

Forgiveness

Faith
Pours from pillars which contain
Accumulated requiems –
A covenant of whispered prayers
Held for half a thousand years,
And from resurrected stone
Ancient psalms and antiphons
Weave a shining weft of peace –
"Agnus Dei qui tollis ..."
I listen in the silence, blest
"Verbum caro factum est".

Agnus Dei qui tollis peccata mundi – Lamb of God, who takest away the sins of the world
Verbum caro factum est – The word is made flesh.

Toc H

My fingers stray
across the keys,
striking the chords
they would have played,
picking up resonances
of Tipperary, and Roses
of Picardy.

Everyman is welcome here.
Cigars and Woodbines mingle
in a mellow cloud,
and diverse accents blend
as Officers and Other Ranks
discover common ground.

In the garden
the peace of flowers
and full-leafed trees
cancels out the barrenness
of battlefields. Hope becomes
the order of the day.

And in the attic-chapel
up a steep and narrow stair,
with an oil-lamp and an altar,
is the healing power
of prayer.

Talbot House (better known by the call-sign "Toc H") was opened in Poperinghe by two army chaplains – Philip (Tubby) Clayton and Neville Talbot – in December 1915. It was unique in that it was an "Everyman's Club" where all Tommies were welcome, not just officers.

There was a library, a lounge/dining-room with a piano, a peaceful garden and, in the attic, a simple chapel. Many soldiers found comfort here, for it provided a "home from home", and a respite from the horrors of war. A chat with Tubby always helped, and many discovered (or rediscovered) their faith here. After the war Talbot House became the centre of the Toc H movement, which exists to foster friendship, service and understanding between people of all races and creeds.

The Altar

The altar was a workbench
Scarred with chisel marks
Where long ago some carpenter,
Skilled at Joseph's craft,
Cut and shaped new furniture
From fine well-seasoned wood,
Took worn damaged pieces
Restored and made them good.

In the war at this same workbench
Knelt broken, empty men,
Seasoned hard with suffering,
Knotted up with pain.
Here another carpenter
Repaired this damaged wood.
With the nails of Jesus' Passion
He restored and made it good.

The Bequest

I opened the box
Of old letters and started
To chip at the chalk-face,
To work my way down.

Like a sapper I tunnelled
Through pain and through sorrow
And there in the depths
Of that redout I found

They'd left me a rich vein
Of love to tap into,
And hope, like bright diamonds,
Lay scattered around,

But beneath was the bedrock
Of faith they bequeathed me,
And now I walk safely
On firm, steady ground.

Peace

The Paris Conference of 1919, which led to the Treaty of Versailles (and the formation of the League of Nations) had more to do with punishing Germany than it did with establishing world peace and international understanding, for the representatives of the countries concerned each had his own agenda.

Clemenceau wanted to weaken Germany's power in order to ensure the safety of France. Lloyd George wanted to secure Britain's economic and political interests. Both paid lip-service to President Wilson's idealistic approach to international order. Wilson was behind the formation of the League of Nations, in which disputes could be settled without resorting to war.

In 1920 Robert E. Greig wrote "... the first great necessity to the tortured world is peace, and it is world peace that the man who knows war wants to see. Peace is a national matter, but more than that it is international. A League of Nations is a beautiful idea, and one that should at least have a fair trial; but its weakness lies in the fact that there can be no guarantee that the nations composing the League may not themselves quarrel."

History has proved his fears were well-founded. He suggested, "The only real solution is the total disarmament of the world, the disbanding of every fighting unit, and the conversion of factories for the manufacture of weapons of war into workshops for the manufacture of the tools of peace. The glamour of war must be killed and the children of the world taught that there is no glamour, only torture and grief, only death and desolation. But these things must be international and world wide, though there is no reason why our school books with their savage glorying in the bloodshed of the past should not now be scrapped and rewritten in such a spirit that the children learning from them might grow up determined that there shall be no more war. That would be a step in the right direction."

Greig's solution, as with the League of Nations, could only succeed in an ideal world. The root problem is that it is not possible to alter the attitudes of all the "children of the world". There will always be those who see war as a means to ends. It is these "ends" (i.e. hunger for power or possessions both on a personal and a national level) which we need to examine and eradicate, along with distrust and suspicion. But we cannot alter human nature ...

Nevertheless, courage, compassion, selfless devotion and hope flourish like beacons in the bleakest scenarios – just as poppies grow best on broken ground.

Unfinished Symphony

The trumpet sounds its shining call
Then drowns beneath the strident swell
Of chords which clash, and clashing grow
To bursting-point, explode and throw
Their shrapnel-shrieks of dissonance
To trembling earth below.

Now silence is more silent
And a darker darkness numbs
All thinking and all feeling
Until softly creeping comes
The keening voice of suffering,
The beat of muffled drums.

And when I think that this is all
Motifs of love resurge and fall
Into the moonless, empty bowl
Of our perpetual night ...
They kindle our hearts' tinder
And bathe our wounds with light.

Encircling us with anthems
They take away our pain
But before the final cadence,
Before the great "Amen"
The seeds of hate and greed spring up
To flourish once again.

And on it goes, the endless loop
Of grief and joy that is the trap –
For we make our own discord
That cannot be resolved
Till every single person
In each corner of the world
Ignores the call to battle
When the flag of war's unfurled

There is no righteous reason,
There's never a just cause
For man to kill his brother.
No war can end all wars ...
I pray in this millenium
Somehow we'll stem the flood
Of violence, for peace can't grow
In pools of human blood.

Flow'rs wither and die
But their seed can lie dormant
For a thousand years.